Michael Davey. 21 JUNE '85. 50p.
(JULY '85)

Is There an Economic Consensus?

Is There an Economic Consensus?

An Attitude Survey

SAMUEL BRITTAN

MACMILLAN

First published 1973 by
THE MACMILLAN PRESS LTD
London and Basingstoke
Associated companies in New York Dublin
Melbourne Johannesburg and Madras

SBN 333 14410 4

Printed in Great Britain by
NORTHUMBERLAND PRESS LTD
GATESHEAD

Contents

Acknowledgements

I must express my warmest gratitude to Professor K. Lumsden and others at the Esmée Fairbairn Economics Research Centre and Mr Arthur L. Welsh of the U.S. Joint Council on Economics Education. Not only did they give me permission to use their questions, without which this survey would have been quite impossible, but at all stages they gave me the optimum combination of help and encouragement with complete freedom to interpret the findings in my own way. They bear, of course, no responsibility for the selection of items for my own questionnaire, nor for the method of assessment I have used, nor for any of the observations or remarks made in this book. Professor Anthony King and David Watt also commented helpfully on the first draft of this work.

1 Introduction

In all matters of opinion and science, the case is opposite; the difference among men is there oftener found to lie in generals than in particulars, and to be less in reality than in appearance. An explanation of the terms commonly ends the controversy: and the disputants are surprised to find that they had been quarrelling, while at bottom they agreed in their judgment.

David Hume, 'Of the Standard of Taste'

Public complaints about disagreements among economists are almost as old as the subject itself. Senior members of the profession still remember the gibe that whenever three economists were gathered together, there were at least four opinions, two of which were Keynes'. More recent jokes on the subject have been less polite.

Differences of opinion among economists seem to cause more indignation than disagreements among theologians, philosophers, art critics, politicians or doctors. One reason for this may be the widespread wishful belief that there exists, away from the clamour of party politics, an impartial expert answer to difficult problems of public policy, a belief that is often held by party politicians themselves. Professional economists often play up to this belief by a clamorous insistence that their subject is, or should be, a science – an insistence which in no way prevents them from engaging in gladiatorial combat in front of the public with a ferocity which makes ordinary party politics seem like a children's parlour game.

The usual way of explaining this state of affairs is to divide *positive economics* – which like any other science states and explains what actually happens in specified circumstances – from the *value judgements* which have to be introduced to draw any conclusions on public policy, and which are necessarily matters of personal opinion. Agreement on positive economics may be difficult because of the complexity of the phenomena and the impossibility of controlled experiments; but data can be collected and rival hypotheses examined without bringing in political ideology or personal preferences.

Simple observation of economic arguments in academic fora, Parliament, or the media, is sufficient to show the inadequacy of the above model. Not only does it fail to account convincingly for disagreement among economists; it cannot explain another phenomenon which is just as widespread, but attracts less attention. This is that economists, despite their well-known squabbles, tend to have some distinctive views on public policy, which mark them out from others in any discussion. Although economists are far from unanimous about subjects such as price competition, tariff protection, farm subsidies, exchange rate changes, or road-space charging, their characteristic and most typical attitudes are very different from those of politicians, journalists or other educated laymen. The differences between economic and lay opinion often cut right across party differences. Some economists tend to emphasise most strongly issues of an 'economists versus laymen' type; others prefer to put the stress on issues dominated by the ordinary political conflict.

The object of the enquiry discussed here was to examine the importance of both the unifying and the divisive factors among the policy views of professional economists, by comparison with the views of politicians and others. I expected that a newcomer to the subject might find himself surprised not only by (a) the extent of disagreement among economists on facts and cause-and-effect relationships but also by (b) the large element of consensus on how to evaluate given facts, cutting to some extent across political lines. Broadly speaking, this expectation was confirmed; but the form of the enquiry threw (b) into more prominence than (a) and also furnished some eminently quotable remarks from some economists who were in a self-conscious revolt against the mainstream thinking of their colleagues.

2 The Enquiry

The enquiry arose through the accident of my coming across some 'objective multiple choice' test questions, designed to test undergraduates. Looking at some of the 'correct' answers it struck me that they might cause surprise, disagreement or even indignation among many laymen and perhaps among some economists. It therefore seemed an interesting experiment to find out how much general assent they commanded among professionals and also to try some of them out among a wider circle of those concerned with public affairs.

Submitting to economists questions originally designed for undergraduates is clearly an indirect way of probing professional opinion, although it is not without its poetic justice. But the alternative of just inventing questions of my own would have been even less satisfactory. The formulation of meaningful multiple choice questions is a complex matter. Many apparently sensible questions contain unexpected snags; and the 'right questions' can only be evolved by a process of trial and error, involving sophisticated discussion of the results. This 'pre-testing' had already been carried out for the tests from which my questions were selected.

Even so their wording was frequently disputed (occasionally in vitriolic terms) by respondents.

There was another, equally important consideration behind the method used. This is that the questions, designed for students, contain answers regarded as 'correct' by an important section of 'mainstream' economists in both the U.K. and the U.S. It is worth exhibiting what these answers are, and comparing them with the responses actually obtained. In this way, something of the nature, extent and limits of any consensus can be examined.

The development and use of specially prepared multiple choice objective tests were the direct outcome of an initiative of the American Economic Association's Committee on Economic Education in 1963. In the U.K., the Associated Examining Board and the University of London have been co-operating in similar endeavours; and since the summer of 1971, such tests have been part of Advanced Level Economics papers. In addition, some universities have used such a test in their first year final economics examinations.

Half the questions selected for the survey on which this paper is based were taken from the *Test of Economics Comprehension* prepared and published by the Esmée Fairbairn Economics Research Centre at the Heriot-Watt University, Edinburgh. Some of these came from an early version of the test published in *Economica* in February 1971,[1] and some from a later version published by the Centre in *Economics Education Project* 2. The test was prepared by the Staff of the Economics Education Project, of which the Director is Professor Keith G. Lumsden and the Research Director Professor Richard Attiyeh.

The remainder of the questions came from the *Test of Understanding in College Economics* prepared by a committee of the U.S. Joint Council on Economic Education. Minimal alterations to the U.S. questions were made, such as the substitution of sterling for dollar figures and the substitution of 'central bank' for 'Federal Reserve' to reduce the specifically American reference. In all the questions, irrespective of source, respondents had to choose between four alternative answers. But in order to give the interested reader an idea of the concept of the 'core' of basic economic knowledge, which lies behind the British objective tests, an extract from a document prepared by K. G. Lumsden and R. E. Attiyeh for the Economics Education Project has been placed at the end of the Appendix.

There seems, in fact, a difference of emphasis between what is claimed for the American and British tests. While the authors of the British tests give the impression that they would like to eliminate value judgements, the U.S. authors of the *Manual to the Test of Understanding in College Economics* argue that complex applications to policy inevitably tend to involve value judgements, and attempts to keep these within the pattern of those generally accepted 'can never be completely successful.'[2]

The supporters of objective tests claim that they can measure 'a substantial amount of student attainment, but not necessarily all of it'. The correlation with success in other forms of examination is less than in, say, mathematics, but higher than in a subject such as history; and correlations of between 0.6 and 0.75 have been reported.[3] The particular tests under discussion aimed deliberately to cover a considerable range of difficulty, and it was not intended that even the better first year students should score anywhere near 100 per cent.

My own study was not concerned with educational controversy about the value of such tests (although naturally there was a little fallout here). The value of the questions for my own investigation was that they were not concerned to test familiarity with economic tools *per se*, but to list applications to 'real life economic situations or problems, identify the economic issues involved and choose the likely outcome or appropriate policy'.

It is only fair to point out that the questions selected were biased in favour of those likely to excite controversy about the 'correct' answers, and are, therefore, not necessarily a representative cross-section of what students are actually asked; indeed, some of the questions included are probably already in the process of being reworded or eliminated for future testing purposes.

3 The Response

The 19 questions listed in the Appendix were sent in the autumn of 1971 to just over 250 economists and usable replies came from 117, which is a very good response rate for enquiries of this kind. The respondents were divided into three categories: 44 academic economists, 37 governmental economists and 21 business economists. (There were 15 anonymous entries whose category could not be traced.) The ratio of these figures was similar to that of the different categories receiving the original questionnaires. The relatively limited number of business economists was a recognition of the hybrid nature of the breed, posed midway between the worlds of academic analysis and business decision. Their inclusion has not had a major impact on the overall results for 'total economists'.

In selecting the academic economists, the names in the *List of Contacts* kindly provided by the Economics Research Centre were first eliminated, as it was important that the questions should be reasonably fresh to the recipients. I also thought it desirable to spare the holders of chairs at the ancient universities this particular form of inquisition. Beyond this, the aim was to combine quality with fair representation of the different universities. For this reason, economists with major published work to their credit stood a greater chance of being picked than did others. Economists working in very specialised applications away from the mainstream of both general theory and public policy were avoided; but a determined attempt was made to obtain a representative cross-section of political and professional opinion. The Appendix contains a list of the great majority of non-Whitehall economists who took part.

The category shown in the table as 'governmental' economists covers not only those employed in Whitehall Departments and the Bank of England at the time of the enquiry, but also a few others with similar background working on similar problems in organisations such as the National Economic Development Office and the National Institute of Economic and Social Research. The views displayed are thus those of a professional category and do not purport to show the advice given to Ministers in the privacy of the confessional. Of the 37 in this category about 30 could be regarded as directly responsible to Ministers; and of these about three-fifths were connected with the Treasury or had related responsibilities. An initial attempt was made to split the whole 37 between those concerned with global economic management problems and those more concerned with 'micro' or environmental problems; but the differences revealed were too small to justify a further sub-division of so limited a sample, except in the case of two questions. The Chief Economic Adviser to the Treasury and his Deputy were spared the inquisition; otherwise the Whitehall recipients covered a broad spread of ranks from junior to very senior positions.

The choice of business economists was the most tricky of all, as those covered by this label range from economists who could easily hold down academic chairs to those who are basically businessmen or City executives who wish to keep in touch with economic discussion. The sample who received questionnaires were chosen partly on the basis of personal reputation and partly because the titles they held in their firms suggested that economic analysis or assessment was a major part of their professional duties.

In addition to the recorded replies, I received notification from 11 who felt unable to take part. One of these was ill; two others turned out to be non-economists in general social studies faculties, and two others had, in fact, been extensively involved in administering multiple choice tests themselves. (One of the non-economists was an economic historian. His replies – although not included – were indistinguishable from the average responses of the economists proper.) This left six who specifically refused to participate. One was opposed in principle to multiple choice questions, two disliked the particular questions received and two decided not to take part because of scepticism about my project. The remaining objector simply asked me if I had stopped beating my wife. (The same question was asked by one other economist who did take part.)

The full text of my accompanying letter is given in the Appendix. It was emphasised that there was no intention of 'testing' economists, but rather of seeing how much agreement there was among them on the 'correct' answers. The U.K. *Test of Economics Comprehension* stated firmly in its instructions to students: 'Blacken only one answer in each question since no question exists where more than one answer is correct.' No such request was included in my own circular letter. It was assumed that respondents knew the general principle of multiple choice questionnaires and that it was undesirable to inhibit them if they felt impelled to answer in terms of more than one option. The circular letter contained the sentences: 'If you feel strongly that any of the questions is too badly phrased to answer, please feel free to say this. But can you please give the test the benefit of the doubt and tick any answer which you think is a reasonable approximation to the truth from the point of view of a student or a member of the general public.' All answers were to be treated as entirely confidential.

As will be readily imagined, a large number of the ticked answers were either rephrased by the respondents or qualified with additional comments; and, in some cases, alternative answers were suggested. One had to strike a compromise between a very rigid treatment to make the answers fit the pre-arranged pigeon holes and the inclusion of so many types of response that all pattern was lost. The additional categories formulated in an attempt to cover fairly the range of responses are displayed with the full questionnaire and replies in the Appendix.

A good deal of judgement was inescapable in the process. Where a respondent made it clear that he regarded the answer he had ticked as the best (or least bad) available, even though he made qualifications or reservations, he was marked accordingly. But if, on the other hand, he made clear the tick was not one in which he had any genuine belief, he was put in the category most closely corresponding to the opinion expressed in his own words. I was particularly concerned, in any doubtful case, to exclude the reply from the 'liberal consensus' answer which I might have personally favoured. Where necessary, I had no hesitation in putting a response in the category labelled 'Impossible to answer on the data and alternatives given'.

The questionnaire was divided into two parts, A and B. The division was to some extent between 'micro' and 'macro' questions. But at least as important in fixing the dividing line was to include, in Part A, questions on which members of the politically interested public might be expected to have views of their own. Part B, on the other hand, contained questions which would be widely regarded as requiring a modicum of professional know-how to answer.

Part A was subsequently sent to a group of M.P.s and political commentators. The significance of any trends which might emerge among economists could be better assessed if they were placed side by side with responses of an alternative reference group, keenly interested in public policy, but without necessarily possessing any sort of economic expertise. The problem with the questionnaire to politicians was that members of the Government could not be expected to reply; and, if the two sides of the House were to be represented on a comparable basis, members of the last Labour Government had also to be largely excluded. A few who held minor Ministerial rank slipped through the net; but they were few enough to compensate for those of comparable calibre and seniority who had for some reason not been included in the Heath Government. To guard against the danger of too heavy a loading in favour of older Members with little prospect of Minis-

terial office, M.P.s shown in the reference books as over
60 were excluded. From then on the pin was the main
instrument used to select just over 100 eligible members from each of the two sides of the House.

Where newspapers had political commentators – or
other columnists on public affairs – these were usually
selected for the sample of 'commentators'. In other cases
the officially designated political correspondent was
chosen. This applied to most of the provincial papers
included. A handful of editors of, or writers on, week-
lies were also sent the questionnaire. (In one case where
the recipient passed on his questionnaire to the chief
specialist economic writer of his paper, the result –
which exhibited with almost perfect accuracy the orthodox liberal economic consensus and was quite untypical
of other journalists – was not included in the computa-
tion.) A few broadcasting producers, interviewers and
others in position of influence were included, but the
great majority of the replies came from practitioners
of the written word.

The political and journalistic recipients were assured
that their identity, as well as their answers, would be
treated as entirely confidential. Some 52 Labour M.P.s
and 39 Conservative M.P.s returned completed questionnaires. A good deal of fascinating information on
attitudes and attitude-clusters among politicians and
commentators emerged as a by-product; and it might
pay some other researcher to probe further into my
data from this point of view.*

* My gratitude should be recorded to all those who took
part, whether economists, politicians or commentators, for the
great trouble to which they went both in completing the questionnaire and in the comments they supplied on the project

There were six letters of refusal from Labour M.P.s and five from Conservatives (excluding a Government Whip who had inadvertently been sent a form). Most of these M.P.s remarked either that they made a habit of not replying to questionnaires, of which they received too many, or that the questions could not usefully be answered by any of the prepared answers. The wittiest was from a Labour Member 'with economic training' who declared that his time was a scarce resource and he was not prepared to devote the several hours thought required to reply in a meaningful way. He was sure I would understand.

---

as a whole and on individual questions. Unfortunately, it was impractical to engage in individual correspondence on all the many interesting points raised at a time when I was coping with more than 300 letters and completed forms; but I hope that the discussion in this work will provide some substitute, however imperfect.

4 The Pattern of Replies

As can readily be imagined, extensive comments were received from economists both on the individual questions and on the survey. A large minority of the economists who replied, especially among the academics (where the proportion was about one in three), expressed reservations of varying strength about the questionnaire as a whole. Adverse criticisms came under two main headings. The first, and probably slightly more frequent, was that the questions were badly, vaguely, ambiguously and loosely drafted and that often none of the answers fitted at all well. This criticism had an echo among a number of M.P.s. In some cases this led to replies in the 'impossible to answer' category and in others to replies that were regarded as merely the least misleading. One economist complained that he was forced to choose between 'painfully second best answers.' A particular variant of this complaint was that not enough information and data were given in the 'stem' of the questions.

One university teacher put the point by saying that the answers could be different 'if different implicit assumptions are made about factors not included as

information in the questions'. The author of this remark showed the questionnaire to two colleagues not
included in my sample and found that such differences
as existed were 'invariably due to different interpreta-
tions of the question' (e.g. whether 'competition', in
Question 6 of Section A, meant perfect competition, or
whether oligopoly was a form of competition). Another
economist, however, strongly supported multiple choice
tests, remarking that 'it does not matter much whether
the questions are ambiguous or not, since the object is
to discuss with the student the reasons why particular
options are invalid or need qualifications'. One specific
criticism was that Section B did not bring out ade-
quately the monetarist versus Keynesian controversy.
Presumably, however, the compilers did not intend to
do this, but to elucidate principles which they hoped
were common to both sides and which were therefore
desirable to emphasise to beginning students.

A second source of complaint was that the questions
were politically loaded and tended to force respondents
into approved political attitudes, or that the range of
answers did not cover certain assumptions that could
have been made. Questions 4, 7 and 8 in Part A were
particularly criticised from this point of view and described by one academic as 'loathsome' queries which
no self-respecting university should pose to its students.
Another economist of similar persuasion complained
that he was forced to particular answers by the terms
of reference. In a few cases, complaints of political loading and of lack of rigour were combined. The most
astringent single letter said that the questionnaire was
an insult to the intelligence of the respondents. Critics
among this school of thought picked particularly on

the use of the concept of 'efficiency' either to conceal certain value judgements or to slide over questions of distribution. Several of the severest critics on such grounds admitted that they found the questions interesting, but objected to the choice of answers. Some of them thought the questions good essay subjects, but unsuitable for 'yes/no' ticks, while others thought that the multiple choice format might be more revealing of students' knowledge and/or economists' attitudes if respondents were required to give a few lines in justification of what they had ticked.

A few economists who made similar criticisms drew a different moral. One eloquent defender of multiple choice questions said that he could often think of contexts in which each of the four postulated answers might be correct; but one could not expect a first-year student to envisage more than the typical case. Another university teacher put the emphasis the other way round, saying that the bad and the good student would both do badly, while the mediocre one would get along on his half knowledge. A handful of respondents, mainly academics, governmental economists and ex-economist Labour M.P.s, remarked that the questionnaire had finally decided them against multiple choice questions as an educational device.

The educational controversy is not the main concern of this paper; but it is possible that the effects of ambiguities, or loose drafting, tend to cancel out, as far as student scores are concerned, if sufficient questions are asked. For what it is worth, the great majority of economic theorists, gave the 'correct' answer to the great majority of the questions that they agreed to answer. But the exact score was valueless as a guide to relative academic distinction. Although some of the most distinguished academics gave the expected answer 90 per cent or more of the time, others, often of equal distinction, scored in the 75–85 per cent range, and, in fact, came slightly behind a number of economists of lesser standing.

Fortunately, the value of this enquiry does not depend on the felicity of the questions for the purposes for which they were originally designed. Indeed many of the fascinating comments received might not have been elicited by more smoothly designed queries. This was, in fact, the view of a good many of even the severest critics of the questions, who ended up by remarking that the results should nevertheless be interesting.

It so happens that I have some sympathy with those who protested against the undefined use of the term 'efficiency' and would (as I have argued elsewhere) prefer to state the case for a liberal economy in somewhat different terms, openly stressing its dependence on certain value judgements, political probabilities and impressionistic empirical generalisations. The critics can legitimately argue that the pattern of answers regarded as 'correct' by the devisors of the test embodies a distinct policy outlook, which, for want of a better label, will be termed the 'liberal economic orthodoxy.' It would be better to admit this fact than to protest too much about the neutrality of the questions. The history of economics is largely that of a running debate between this liberal economic orthodoxy and its critics; the characteristic achievements of the latter have been to point out the weaknesses of the liberal orthodoxy (which is perhaps now more convincingly formulated as a result) rather than to outline a convincing alternative.

Be that as it may, the reader can best form his own impression of the contents of the liberal economic orthodoxy by looking first at the answers marked as 'correct' in the full table of questions and replies given in the Appendix. *The characteristic belief that emerges from these 'correct' answers is that competitive markets and the pursuit by individuals of their own interests can – with definable exceptions – produce an effective and prosperous economic system, and a reasonable harmony between public and private interest. Although such a harmony can be provided by a competitive capitalist system, the key to success is not ownership, but freely operating competitive markets, which can also be envisaged in a socialist economy where enterprises are state-owned. Free markets, however, will not necessarily bring about a desirable distribution of income (although what that is, is a matter of personal judgement). But the way to improve distribution is by direct cash grants and taxes or improvement of opportunities rather than by interfering in the market place.*

Such interference can sometimes be justified, but for a totally different purpose. The market works effectively only if enterprises and individuals pay for all the costs that their activities impose on the rest of the community and if a price is charged for all benefits conferred. Where there are costs, such as pollution by automobile exhaust or factory waste products, for which those responsible do not pay, or where benefits are conferred for which it is impracticable to make individual charges, state interference is then necessary. But this interference is best achieved by adjusting rela-

*tive prices through taxes and subsidies – and on occa-
sion by the state provision of services – rather than by
direct controls or prohibitions.*

Subscribers to this outlook would accept that considerable unemployment can exist because of the slow-
ness of wages and prices to respond to changing supply
and demand conditions. But they clearly believe that
this is a fact of life and that slumps and booms are best
controlled by global demand management. They adopt
the middle-of-the road position that both monetary and
fiscal policy can affect total demand, but are sufficiently
Keynesian to believe that demand management is
likely, over quite a long period, to affect real output
and employment and not just money incomes and
prices.

Despite the various reservations already noted, the
replies and comments suggest that the above outlook is
shared by well over 75 per cent of the economists who
took part in this survey – except on the question of
housing to which nearly half of those replying had
qualms about applying the liberal orthodox approach.
Among the minority of respondents who rejected the
whole outlook, there were those who described it as
'right' or 'neo-classical' or inspired by that pro-market
body, the Institute of Economic Affairs. A glance at the
responses of politicians to Section A will, however, show
that the liberal orthodox outlook is as far removed from
that of most Conservative M.P.s as it is from most
Labour ones.

A large number of economists, even among those
who voted fairly solidly for the liberal orthodox ticket,
showed an extreme pre-occupation with the distribution of income – arguably outrivalling that of many

Labour M.P.s. An impressionistic judgement is that their egalitarian concern is greater than among economists in most other Western countries, and greater than that of almost any other British middle class professional group outside the social sciences. If one were to redefine concern with the distribution of income to mean *general* as distinct from *specific* egalitarianism, then I would hazard the guess that there is greater support for this among economists even than among other social scientists with a far more 'trendy left' reputation. Such economists are prepared to compromise in order to achieve other desirable goals such as prosperity, but regard equality rather than 'payment according to merit' as their ethical ideal. It is often forgotten that the archetypally orthodox Victorian economist, Alfred Marshall, actually believed it to be demonstrable that the satisfaction derived from a given quantity of income would be maximised if it were equally distributed – although he found hundreds of reasons for extreme caution in applying this belief to policy.

The merits and drawbacks of the egalitarian form of the puritan legacy are not the concern of this book.* The relevant point is that whether or not an economist was prepared to subscribe to the liberal orthodoxy often depended on whether he was prepared to treat questions of the allocation of resources on their own merits, in the belief that any major undesired effect on the distribution of income could be offset, or more than offset, by the tax and social security system (as well as by more fundamental policies designed to improve educational opportunities and remove monopolistic re-

---

* They are discussed in the companion volume, *Capitalism and the Permissive Society*, pp. 124 et seq.

trictions on entry into occupations). The view of the minority of dissentient economists was that – despite the ample opportunities of testifying to the importance they attached to income redistribution in Questions A4, A8, B1 and above all B2 – it was impossible to make any judgement about any aspect of the allocation of resources or of economic organisation without taking specific account of distribution; and the fiercest objection to the whole questionnaire project came from among this school of thought. Some objectors were mainly concerned with hypothetical logical possibilities. But there were also genuine fears that liberal orthodox measures for improving allocation or increasing consumer choice would have important distributional effects, which might not tend to cancel out, but could well be adverse and outweigh the other benefits claimed for them. This outlook also implies a very great scepticism about the feasibility or likelihood of fiscal offsets for undesired distributional changes – either for technical and administrative reasons, or because of the moral failings of elected Governments.

It would be quite wrong incidentally to suppose that all 'left-wing' economists shared in the violent reaction exhibited by a few. One highly respected theorist, passionately concerned with distributional questions and very suspicious of the unadulterated market mechanism, remarked that most of the questions seemed totally innocuous and asked whether there really would be disagreement. A number of economists of pronounced Labour or Lib–Lab sympathies, both in the universities and in Whitehall, found no difficulty in subscribing to what I have termed the liberal orthodoxy – in many cases even in the question on housing. The kind of economist most liable to erupt was one who *combined* strong left-wing views on distribution and capitalist free markets with an extreme dedication to econometric method, and/or an insistence on the impossibility of generalising about second best solutions according to the most rigorous standards of static welfare economics.

In any case, no respondent was forced to answer the questions in terms of a liberal orthodoxy of which he disapproved. The economists in question were not born yesterday; and by either not ticking the 'expected' answer, or by adding appropriate comments, they successfully ensured that their replies were not placed in a category they disliked. I shudder to think, however, what this enquiry would have yielded if it had been undertaken by the fashionable computerised methods, in which only rigidly pre-specified alternatives would have been digested by a literal-minded magnetic tape incapable of reading marginal comments, or accompanying letters of very varying style, form and length.

5 Politicians and Economists

The reader might find it interesting to compare the distribution of economists' responses in Part A with those of M.P.s. Even an impressionistic glance is sufficient to show that differences between economists are, in most cases, very much less than the differences between economists taken together and politicians taken together. This is so whether the comparison is with Labour or Conservative M.P.s or an average of the two parties. *Moreover where politicians were attracted by supposedly 'incorrect' answers, the direction of the deviation was more often than not very similar for both Labour and Conservative Members.* Nor can this be entirely explained by saying that economists 'know more' about the subjects than the M.P.s or are more expert in interpreting the questions. The topics covered are not esoteric problems of monetary policy but are mostly down-to-earth problems of rush hour traffic, smog-prevention, housing policy, the effects of competition on profits and social harmony, the workings of state socialism or the effects of size in business. These are all matters on which politicians have beliefs

both about cause-and-effect relations and about what
ought to be done.

The differences between them and the economists
may reflect inadequate knowledge on the part of either
side, different value judgements, or more subtle differences in the concepts with which the world is viewed.
These differences lead to striking contrasts in diagnoses
and policy conclusions. To the extent that they reflect
different value judgements, this too is interesting. For
value judgements do not always arrive from heaven;
and the kind of learning experience accumulated by a
politician tends to produce a different outlook on
'ought' questions from that accumulated by the typical
economist. Another factor, however, may be that those
who stick to economics as a career may tend from the
outset to have different value judgements from those
who are more attracted to – or more liable to be successful in – politics.

The application of the price mechanism to public
transport, for instance, attracted the great majority of
economists but was accepted by a minority even of Conservative M.P.s and by an even smaller minority of
commentators. Economists are interested in the price
mechanism as a short-term rationing device, and still
more as a method of allocating resources in the longer
run in relation to the revealed preferences of individual
consumers when they know the true relative costs of
the different alternatives. Economists who are critical
of the working of capitalism emphasise the possible adverse effects of short term rationing by price on poorer
people, and are suspicious that many of the true costs
and benefits do not enter into the longer term pricing
decisions of private enterprise. But politicians have,

for the most part, no such belief in the value of the price mechanism, even when adapted to compensate for the above mentioned defects. The question on housing showed that, not merely did an overwhelming majority of Labour M.P.s disagree with the liberal orthodox answer, but that a greater percentage even of Conservative M.P.s supported below cost housing for the poor, in preference to cash subsidies, than did professional economists.

Having said so much about liberal orthodoxy in the economic sense, it might be worth looking at the replies of M.P.s who were 'Liberal' with a capital 'L'. Unfortunately the three replies constituted too small a sample to include in the tabulation. Generalisation was made even more difficult by the great divergence among the three Liberal M.P.s. There was not a single question where all three ticked the same reply. On some topics two of them did agree, but it was not the same two from one question to another.

It is therefore scarcely surprising that one of the Liberal M.P.s wrote a very engaging accompanying letter saying that – although he was making a personal exception in my case – he believed it was 'immoral to encourage this type of questionnaire.' Not long ago he discovered 'a very nice Associate Professor from an American university' spending a whole summer examining the power structure in one of the remote rural fringes of the U.K. The professor produced a list of 100 questions in which he asked the local hill farmers 'about such questions as socialised medicine and the war in Vietnam, to which they duly recorded the answers they thought he would like'.

If one can risk a broad observation from the two most

senior and best known of the Liberal M.P.s, it is that they were further from the liberal economic attitudes than most economists, but a good deal nearer to them than the typical Labour or Conservative M.P. They may both be sorry to learn that the whole profile of their replies was also markedly closer to the Conservative than the Labour pattern.

To sum up briefly the reasons for the differences between economists' and politicians' replies, two factors may be advanced. The first, and more prosaic, one is that practical politicians find it more difficult to think in terms of assumptions and hypotheses and tend to answer as if they were asked an immediate question on U.K. policy.

Secondly – and far more interesting – most economists have some sort of intellectual commitment to the price mechanism, at least as a tool of economic policy, even when they are strong opponents of laissez-faire. Politicians, on the other hand, do not have any particular sympathy for prices as an allocative device and, like the general public, have some difficulty in distinguishing between relative prices and the general price level.

Sweeping conclusions about commentators' attitudes prove surprisingly difficult. No pronounced 'trendy left' tendency was apparent, perhaps because of the low representation of television and the relatively high representation of provincial political correspondents. The profile of journalistic responses did resemble more closely that of Labour than of Conservative M.P.s, but not by an enormous margin, or on all questions. For example, journalists were much less sceptical than Labour M.P.s about the beneficial effects of price com-

petition in pushing down prices, and joined whole-
heartedly with the Conservatives in accepting the
conventional view of the supposed advantages of size
in business.

In the majority of questions a somewhat greater proportion of journalists than of M.P.s of either party gave
the liberal orthodox 'correct' answer. But simply looking at numbers and percentages here is misleading. The
most sensitive question for economic liberals (A7),
showed that commentators had little belief in the poten-
tialities of the market mechanism; over 70 per cent
supported below cost public housing for poor persons
in preference to cash grants, and more commentators
than even Labour M.P.s believed that 'the presumed
harmony' between individual and public interest depended on planning from the centre. The main reason
why the commentators achieved a higher average score
of 'correct' answers than M.P.s was that they avoided
the worst partisan absurdities, such as calling for lower
fares at peak hours, ticking political catch-phrases that
were irrelevant to the question posed, and displaying
emotional attitudes to S.E.T. In addition, their strong
feelings about the environmental effects of pollution
and motor cars led them to standard economists' answers
– although not necessarily by the same route.

Altogether the commentators emerged as sound,
common sense people, sensitive to obvious social costs,
highly sceptical of party political exaggeration or
slogan-mongering, and wedded to the post-war form of
the welfare state. They were, if anything, less in touch
than the politicians with the debate that has ranged
over the past two hundred years on the strengths and
weaknesses of the market as a major human institution,

although their lack of partisan blinkers may have compensated for this when it came to specific issues. But they seemed on this evidence unlikely to be very active in stimulating unconventional thoughts of any hue on the way we run our affairs. These are, of course, generalisations to which there are many individual exceptions, but they are supported by Jeremy Tunstall's independent findings from which political and lobby correspondents (as distinct from labour ones) emerge as fairly evenly distributed in their political partisanship. The majority wanted to spend more on education and 'welfare' and less on 'Whitehall administration and defence'. Among specialist correspondents in general this fairly uncritical support for the post-war welfare state was combined with a healthy scepticism about spending public money on spectacular prestige projects (despite their news value). 'Economic' planning and 'Government assistance to industry' were also unpopular.[4]

6 Transport and Pollution

At this stage of the analysis it is no longer possible to proceed any further without question-by-question examination of responses.

The first question in Section A asked how tube and bus fares should vary during the day to make 'the most efficient use of a city's resources.' The 'correct' answer was intended to be that 'they should be relatively high during rush hour to minimise the amount of equipment needed to transport the daily travellers'. The reasoning presumably was that each additional peak hour passenger, when existing services were already fully utilised, would mean additional investment in vehicles and other items of capital equipment. On the other hand, additional passengers at off-peak periods add only to the running costs of existing vehicles. Thus the more traffic that can be switched to off-peak periods, the smaller the stock of vehicles and other equipment required to provide services of any given standard.

Some 88 per cent of the economists accepted the orthodox answer as at least a reasonable approximation to the truth. But this was one of the very few

questions when there was a notable difference between
'governmental' economists concerned with 'micro'
or environmental problems and those of a more
'Treasury' orientation. While the latter group overwhelmingly supported the orthodox answer, a substantial minority of the former group – who might be
regarded as nearer the actual problem – dissented or
expressed reservations. By far the most frequent objection was that ordinary money calculations took no
account of the additional costs in congestion, pollution
and the like that would be imposed by any diversion
of rush hour passengers to private cars.

The question was ambiguous on whether a 'city's
resources' meant the public transport services alone,
or was a wider concept including roads and the general
environment. Even so, the point about road congestion was at least partly covered by the expression 'relatively high' in the 'correct' answer. There was
therefore nothing to stop the authorities subsidising
public transport sufficiently to bring down fares at all
times, but making them specially cheap (or even free) at
off-peak periods. It is certainly possible to imagine an
extreme case where the number of private commuter
cars was highly sensitive to the level of public transport fares, but there was very little elasticity between
peak and off-peak travel in relation to the fare structure. I suspect that this is a short term view that ignores
the eventual responsiveness of employers to the desires
of their personnel to adjust their working hours in
such a situation; but the possibility of such a perverse
situation is there.

In contrast to the economists, nearly 80 per cent of
Labour M.P.s, over 60 per cent of Conservatives and

most commentators were definitely opposed to relatively high peak fares. Their marginal comments did not suggest that they had such perverse elasticities in mind – or even that their answers were due to overlooking the word 'relatively'. In most cases they did not even consider the use of relative prices as an instrument of allocation. They thought it 'fair' that travellers should pay the same at all times irrespective of the fact that they were buying different services with different underlying costs. One Tory M.P., however, suggested that the compiler of the question had never been a bus conductor and asked him to imagine the confusion if someone joined a bus queue at an off-peak period, only to find the bus arriving after the changeover.

The questionnaire reached M.P.s (although not economists) at the time of the rumpus over the large increase in London Transport fares in the winter of 1971/2, a rumpus which coincided with a campaign for free urban public transport. A large number of Labour M.P.s added remarks advocating zero or very low fares for tubes and buses. This is not a case that can be dismissed *a priori* even on liberal orthodox assumptions, whatever one's views on its empirical plausibility. Some 40 per cent of the Labour M.P.s however (but none of the Tories), advocated as their first choice, or as a second best to 'free transport', that fares should be differentially *low* during rush hours. Although one could invent certain extreme assumptions about differential elasticities of substitution between public and private transport at peak and off-peak hours, which, together with other extreme assumptions about the ratio of private to social cost in the two forms of transport, would justify this view, it would be straining credulity to suppose that this is what these M.P.s had in mind – even implicitly. The main belief involved seemed to be that all prices should be as low as possible for as many people as possible, but above all for 'workers', and this can be rationalised by saying that they believed in using particular prices to bring about certain desired shifts in the distribution of income irrespective of the effects on the allocation of resources. (These desired shifts are not necessarily egalitarian, as pensioners and non-working housewives would be among the worst hit by a differential subsidy for peak hour travellers.)

What many Labour M.P.s seemed to overlook was that subsidy of public transport was not the only way of bringing the relative prices of private and public transport into line with their relative social costs. The alternative is some form of 'congestion tax' which would make the urban motorist pay the full cost of bringing his car into town; and this alternative would have the advantage of avoiding a subsidy on mere movement. As a well known Oxford economist stressed, the orthodox answer of higher peak hour fares would be correct if private motoring were 'priced correctly'.

Question 2 of Section A caused far less analytical difficulty. Respondents were asked to suppose that smog, caused by automobile exhaust, could be largely eliminated by erecting a large number of small air purification plants. The problem was why it was unlikely to pay private firms to erect such plants. The 'correct' answer was that, in contrast to other marketable services, smog-free air could not be sold to those willing to pay for it, but withheld from others. Some of the other suggested reasons were also possibilities, and were mentioned by economists of distinction; but the inability to market smog-free air is decisive and 88 per cent of the economists mentioned it, either alone, or together with one of the others. Two thirds of the M.P.s in both parties had no difficulty in spotting this as the main reason why the market forces could not cope with the problem unaided.

Question 3, which asked how such purification plants should be financed to secure efficiency in the allocation of resources, was far more controversial. Taxes on motor vehicle fuel, general sales, property and income were all four suggested as possibilities. Motor fuel tax was meant to be the 'correct' answer – presumably because the number and running costs of the plants were related to motor vehicle use; and the owner of a vehicle therefore imposed an additional cost on the city roughly in proportion to his fuel consumption. The majority of economists giving the favoured response was distinctly less than in the case of the previous two questions – although it was 75 per cent if those mentioning one other tax as well are included. The dissenters had vigorous and well-argued objections. A few economists opted for property, because they took for granted the present British institutional structure, which restricts the range of local taxes, and regarded property ownership as roughly correlated with use of motor vehicles. But the majority took the question (which was of U.S. origin) in the hypothetical spirit intended.

The simplest objection to the fuel tax was that, as it was merely a city tax, people would buy their petrol outside. Alternatively, if the fuel tax were inescapable, but there was no smog problem on country roads, there would, as one industrial economist pointed out, be an unnecessary deterrent to out-of-town driving. Another objection from a similar quarter was that the fuel tax might be the most suitable were it not for the fact that petrol was already too highly taxed!

Some strict theorists made the much more general point that unless the four kinds of taxes were already at 'optimum' levels, nothing could be said about which of them should be raised to pay for the purification plants. This is not the place to tackle the general question of the second best; but one cannot resist remarking that if economists opt out of issues where first best solutions are not feasible, because they cannot offer arguments of sufficient rigour, the field will be left entirely free to others who will have no such scruples about the stringency of their logic. A less absolutist approach would be to say that, on the assumptions envisaged in the question, a motor fuel tax would be appropriate if it could be raised without avoidance; but that if there were already strong reasons for changing the tax balance in a different direction, then these might outweigh the particular arguments for charging motor vehicles for the purification plants.

The most ingenious argument of all came, of course, from an Oxford economist who argued that if the distribution of taxes had been correct in the first place, then motor fuel tax should actually be *reduced* when the purification plants were built. This was because, under a proper pricing system, the motorist would pay for the disamenity or social costs imposed by his exhaust fumes. But once the air is purified this particular reason for taxing and discouraging motor use

would vanish! *Provided that* the additional purification costs arising from each additional vehicle mile is
less than the damage and discomfort originally caused
by the fumes, the argument seems unassailable.

Nearly 50 per cent of M.P.s in both parties voted
for the motor fuel tax, singly or in combination, as a
way of financing the purification plants – more than
for any other single alternative. The lesser degree of
support, compared with economists, hardly calls for
comment in view of the vigorous professional discussion on whether the motor tax really was the right
answer. More noteworthy was that M.P.s and commentators found it much more difficult than the economists
to accept Questions 2 and 3 as dealing with a deliberately hypothetical situation. They tended much more
to challenge the assumptions (which were, of course,
not intended to be realistic) and to plunge in with
their own views on automobile exhaust devices and
local government finance. Sometimes this resulted in
a refusal to contemplate any of the alternatives, but
slightly more often in insertions of additional remarks.
Particularly remarkable was the number of Conservative M.P.s who were convinced that the answer was the
compulsory fitting of some anti-fume device attached
to cars, thereby illustrating the party's penchant (con-
trary to popular belief) for physical intervention in
preference to price mechanism devices.

A large number of M.P.s treated the financing of
the anti-pollution plants simply as a problem of finding additional revenue. If one looks at where the ticks
fell of those who did not support a higher motor duty,
one gets a revealing glimpse into party attitudes. In
the secrecy of the confessional a considerable body of

Labour M.P.s favoured raising income tax for the purpose – an option which found far fewer takers among the Tories. A smaller, but still substantial, body of Conservatives were attracted by a general sales tax, a course which raised an even chillier response among Labour M.P.s.

7 The Housing Furore

The question of Section A that raised the real hornets' nest was Number 4, which asked recipients to evaluate below-cost public housing to poor persons, compared to a direct social security payment. There was here a dramatic drop in support for the liberal orthodoxy even among economists. The approved answer (b), that it is 'less efficient because it will result in too much housing and too little of the other things consumers want', received a bare 51 per cent support from the economists polled. Even the inclusion of additional or alternative reasons for preferring the direct social security payment produced a percentage of only 58 per cent opposed to below-cost housing.

This was a question where, to obtain meaningful results, some interpretation of the concept of efficiency on my own part was unavoidable. Efficiency relates to achieving a chosen goal at minimum cost, or to maximising the amount of some chosen objective that can be achieved for a given cost. If satisfying the preferences of consumers is not accepted as a desirable goal then a housing system that fails to reflect these preferences cannot thereby be condemned as inefficient.

There is not a mystical quantity called economic efficiency which can be maximised irrespective of the values and goals of the person making the judgement. For this reason I excluded from the category of those endorsing the answer (b) desired by the test compilers, not merely those who put their tick in another place, but also those who did tick this answer but qualified it by some remark indicating that they did not really believe it, or that 'economic' considerations should give way to 'social', or remarks of a similar bent. On the other hand, those who merely expressed some reservations, indicating that the approved answer might be subject to qualification or exception, were regarded as voting for it 'as a reasonable approximation to the truth' in the spirit of the accompanying letter.

Why then the breakaway from liberal orthodoxy by economists who were willing to accept it on other questions? On this question there was an interesting difference between the business economists and the others. Not only was there very much *less* support for replacing subsidised housing by cash grants among the business economists, but they were avowedly more paternalistic about their reasons. One-third supported below-cost public housing for reason (c), because subsidies of this form could not 'be spent on undesirable goods such as tobacco and drink'. Only a trivial proportion of academic and governmental economists, M.P.s and commentators were prepared to offer this reason; the straightforwardness of the business economists was indeed a refreshing contrast to the rationalisations offered by others.

Some economists, who formed quite a small minority in the sample, but were nevertheless distressingly too many for a liberal, indicated that they did not accept, even as a general principle, the fulfilment of consumer preferences as a criterion of efficiency. A rather larger minority wanted to make a paternalistic exception in the case of housing. Apart from general references to 'socially acceptable' minimum standards or to an alleged distinction between wants and needs, a variety of *ad hoc* reasons were given for rejecting consumer choices in this particular field. There were references to lack of consumer information, and the costs of acquiring it. One economist spoke of 'indivisibilities in the housing stock' which were supposed to rule out any intermediate possibility between the amount of national spending on housing now achieved by the subsidy system and a catastrophic dive in standards. There were also references to the 'interdependence of the utility functions' of the rich and the poor, which – translated out of jargon – seems to mean the same as Shaw's remark that the slums should be pulled down because the sight of them distressed him. There were also some cryptic references to 'externalities'. Apart from being yet another way of referring to the effect on some people's aesthetic sensibilities of low standard housing, respondents sometimes had in mind deficiencies in the organisation of either the building industry or housing finance – but for this to be plausible such deficiencies would not merely have to exist, but to be such as to be remediable or offset by the provision of subsidised public housing.

There were, however, two objections to the orthodox answer which could not be brushed aside by the most thorough-going believer in freedom of choice. One economist who disliked the paternalist attitude claimed

that there were still practical snags in the negative
income tax idea, which would be required to make
cash grants an effective substitute; another pointed out
that if the choice of how much to spend on accommodation was made by the head of the household this might
not reflect the desires of the other members of the
family.

Having said this, I do not think that the reasons
offered fully explain the extent or force of the revolt
against the orthodox answer on the housing question.
My own guess is that many economists were suspicious
of being trapped into subscribing to some form of
'free market' or 'IEA-type' manifesto. To most questions they gave the answer that would professionally
be expected; but when they came to as politically
charged a subject as homes for the poor, they dug in
their heels and were determined to provide no com-
fort to the opponents of subsidised council building.

There was probably another more sophisticated
element in this revolt. Although the question specifically guaranteed the preservation of at least the existing element of redistribution, by stipulating that
housing subsidies would be replaced by cash grants,
there may well have been suspicion that in any
thorough-going reform there would be some reverse
redistribution in favour of middle or upper class taxpayers. Nor is this unreasonable. A glance at the political responses shows the overwhelming support for
the traditional subsidised council housing approach
among Labour M.P.s; so that reform of the liberal
orthodox variety would be politically extremely difficult for any but a Conservative Government. Nor could
the respondents forget completely the actual housing

proposals just then announced by the Secretary of State. These were of course very different from those suggested by the liberal orthodox reply. There was no suggestion of introducing a free market in housing rents combined with untied cash grants for the less well off. On the other hand, the Conservative Government's proposals did represent a move away from the traditional post-war system, and the proposed income-graduated rebates for both council and private tenants did have more of a flavour of direct social security payments than the previous concept of a council rent. Moreover, the new policy was meant to lead to a financial saving by the Treasury; and it was a fair presumption that some of this would find its way back to taxpayers with a higher income on average than the council tenants whose rents had been raised.

Of course it was possible – and in my view likely – that the redistribution would be in more than one direction; that there would be a redistribution *both* towards some of the poorest families living in privately rented accommodation, who previously obtained no rebate, *and* towards the middle and upper classes, at the expense of the better off half of the council tenants. This underlines the distinction between concern for raising the standards of the poor and a desire to limit the incomes of the better off as part of an overall egalitarian goal.

When we come to the politicians' replies to the housing question, the response of the Labour M.P.s was all too predictable. Some 80 per cent supported below-cost public housing despite the reference to direct social security payments as an alternative. It is on the Conservative side that the interest lies. For, despite

all that has been said above about the revolt of economists against the liberal orthodoxy on this question,
a higher proportion of Conservative M.P.s – 38 per
cent – than of economists positively favoured below-
cost public housing. (Some of the economists who
revolted against the orthodox answer declared the question impossible to answer in the terms posed.)

Moreover, even among those Conservatives who
came out against below-cost public housing, the most
widely supported was that 'the Government cannot
manage housing efficiently'. Of course, excessive provision of housing for council tenants compared with
what they might freely choose under a cash subsidy
system is not the only – or perhaps even the main –
distortion of the housing market arising from the
traditional approach to housing policy; and, in the
case of *politicians and commentators only*, the interpretation of the 'correct' answer was stretched to
include any adverse distortion of the housing market
other than the generalised charge of public enterprise
inefficiency. Even on this broad interpretation barely
more than a quarter of the Tories mentioned the
'correct' answer, either on its own or with others.

The fifth question of Section A, which asked about
the most important economic function of rental payments for the use of land, saw a great rush back to
orthodoxy. The great majority of the economists,
including 96 per cent of the academics, ticked the
intended reply that it was 'to influence how land will
be used.' The use of prices to allocate scarce resources
to the sectors where they yield the highest return is
probably the most important single element of
common ground on policy questions among econo-

mists; and, as the question left completely open who
would own the land, to what extent the rents should
be taxed, or even whether they should be controlled
or determined by the market, there was little scope
for any of the usual objections to the price mechanism
approach. (Even here, however, one academic economist complained of 'the lack of consideration for distributional issues' and said he could envisage situations
where the allocation of land among alternative uses
was less important than the effect of land rents on the
distribution of income.)

The M.P.s' answers were, on the other hand, all
over the place and did not relate in any discernible
way to party affiliation or ideological position. The
cause of this formless scatter was that two of the other
suggested answers – that the economic function of rents
was 'to ensure owners some return for its use' and 'to
assure an adequate supply of land in the society as a
whole' – could hardly be said to be wrong; and the
teleological form of the question was bound to be con-
fusing to those unfamiliar with the economists'
ingrained approach. The contrast between the two sets
of responses does bring out how foreign the economists'
view of the role of prices (and land rent is, of course,
a price) is to the normal politician's (or ordinary
citizen's) way of thinking.

8 Public and Private Interests

In the sixth question, respondents were asked about the truth or falsity of the following statements about a private enterprise economy:

(a) One of the principal effects of competition is to force prices to the lowest level consistent with normal profits.

(b) One of the principal functions of profits is to indicate to the government where wages are too low.

Some 83 per cent of the economists accepted that (a) was true and virtually none accepted (b). The remaining minority did not accept the truth of either proposition. The explanation given in the *Interpretive Manual* for the correctness of statement (a) is that if, owing to increased demand, the production of a good becomes highly profitable, firms will try to take 'advantage of this by producing more of that good; but only if there is competition will firms fully accommodate consumers' preferences by expanding output to the point where consumers' valuation just matches the cost (including normal profit) of production.'

In common with a few of the respondents, I was a little unhappy about the concept of 'normal profits', the rate of which is itself unexplained. But for operational purposes it can be taken, as one business economist put it, as the minimum rate of return required to keep a company in business in the medium to long run. Much the most frequent point raised by those who rejected or qualified assertion (a) was that it depended on competition being 'perfect' competition. The term 'perfect competition' seems to bring with it a mare's nest of confusion. It is something of a misnomer. For it does not mean 'best possible', 'most highly developed' or 'best functioning' form of competition, but refers simply to a market – such as prevails in some metals and grains – where the individual seller faces an infinitely high elasticity of demand for his product. If he raises his price by the tiniest of fractions, he will lose all his customers, while, if he were to drop however slightly below the going price, he would be overwhelmed by unmanageable floods of orders.

There are many kinds of market situations which are not perfect in this sense, but where free entry alone will bring in enough competitive supplies to keep profits down to 'normal' levels. The retail trade is light years removed from perfect competition, yet the free entry of competitors is sufficient to bring profits down to normal levels for firms of average entrepreneurial efficiency. There is more room for genuine controversy about *prices* being 'at the lowest level consistent with ...' Doubtless, if there were no new products, if consumer desires were standardised and it were considered unethical to influence them by sales propaganda, and if the lowest cost methods of production were already known, then either perfect competition, or state action to simulate its effects, would be an improvement on the type of competition that can actually exist at present. But merely to state these conditions is to show the irrelevance of the concept.

The obsession with perfect competition is one of the biggest weaknesses of British undergraduate economic education, especially (I get the impression) in one of the older universities. This is very unfortunate, because all is far from the best in real life, the degree of competition and its effectiveness differ enormously from one market to another, and there is a vast reform agenda awaiting any government genuinely interested in promoting competition. But talk of perfect competition simply detracts attention from the relevant issues. The concept has its role as a useful simplifying assumption in certain areas of economic discourse; but public policy towards business is not one of them.

As will be readily imagined the vast majority of Conservative M.P.s found no difficulty in ticking statement (a), whatever precise interpretation they put upon it. It was also endorsed by just over 40 per cent of the Labour M.P.s. This probably means that, even if competition was not their ideal system, they conceded that it had some beneficial effect on prices and profits – or was at least a lesser evil than its absence in a private enterprise economy. But well over half the sample were not even prepared to go that far.

The most encouraging aspect of this question, however, was that hardly any Labour M.P. or commentator fell into the trap of regarding profits as primarily an index of where wages were too low. Such an approach would not only be the biggest imaginable deterrent to good and imaginative management, but it would also have led to vast new inequities between different groups of workers. One wonders how this question would have been answered by trade union leaders or a general sample of voters and heaves a sigh of relief at the absence of direct democracy.

Question 7 in Part A is a good example of how an ambiguously worded question can nevertheless produce informative responses. Four alternative possibilities were given on which 'the presumed harmony between individual and public interest' depended 'in a free enterprise economy.' The intended answer was 'competitive markets and pursuit of self-interest by individuals.'

Because of the expression 'presumed harmony' a number of respondents were puzzled about whether they were being examined in the economic theory of the 'invisible hand', or being asked for their own judgement about what actually happens today. One can sympathise with those Labour M.P.s who, together with a few economists, scribbled in 'Presumed by whom?' or something similar. It was also far from clear whether or not it could be assumed that official action was being taken to make sure that proper prices were put on those 'external', 'spillover' or 'neighbourhood' costs and benefits which remain unpriced under laissez-faire.

About 80 per cent of the academic and governmental economists accepted that the presumed harmony depended upon competitive markets. One academic economist crossed out 'and pursuit of self interest' from the phrase beginning 'competitive markets'. This was understandable, because the success of a competitive free enterprise economy, working under the right environmental policies, depends on people pursuing *self-chosen* interests, which can be altruistic, aesthetic or anything else; and it is only to give away the game unnecessarily to the dirigistes to imply that it depends on narrowly self-centred conduct by narrow 'economic men.'

One of the possible answers provided in the question was 'a strong desire for profit maximisation.' This was not regarded as correct by the test compilers, presumably because this could lead to perverse results in the absence of sufficiently competitive markets. But there is a case for saying that such a desire is at least a necessary, if not a sufficient condition, for the vigorous and effective supplying of consumer needs and for economic growth (if that is desired).

The main interest of this question lies in the identity of the dissentients. A surprisingly large minority of Labour M.P.s – over one-quarter – indeed ticked 'competitive markets' and/or 'profit maximisation' when they had the opportunity of voting for 'careful planning and co-ordination of economic activity'. This probably means that they were answering in terms of a 'presumed' harmony in which they did not believe. Much more impressive is the fact that somewhat less than half of the Conservative M.P.s attributed this harmony to competitive markets, either alone or in conjunction with profit maximisation. Some 14 per cent attributed it to profit maximisation alone; but these were outnumbered by the 28 per cent who voted either for 'careful planning' or for 'social responsibility by private businessmen.' Two or three Conservative M.P.s and one very prominent Liberal thought it wrong to plump for any one or two of the four alternatives as the *only* factors upon which harmony between individual and public interest depended. They insisted that a mixture of all four was required, plus, in the view of the Liberal, 'greater social responsibility by Government and local authority officials.' Among the business economists too, the view that the harmony depended on competitive markets was noticeably less frequent than among their academic or governmental colleagues. Whatever may be alleged against the liberal economic orthodoxy, the charge that it is either the Tory Party or Big Business in disguise seems singularly ill-conceived.

9 Socialist Economics

Question 8 of Section A went into different territory. It started with a long quotation about reforms in Soviet bloc countries which were said to have brought back free price competition in the market, for all commodities except a few staples which would retain centrally fixed prices. The countries concerned had shattered the rigidity of central planning 'as there was no other way out of their problems.' Alternative comments were offered on this state of affairs. Unfortunately the question did not ask which of the comments was true, but which represented the view of 'many Western economists.' There was also a failure to define socialism except in the most implicit terms. But close inspection of both the percentages and the comments received suggested that this complication made surprisingly little difference to the result.

About three-quarters of the economists agreed that the quotation supported the view that 'a freely-operating market system can perform efficiently the function of allocating scarce resources to satisfy competing wants under socialism as well as under capitalism.' This view may be optimistic, as I have argued elsewhere, but the other possible answers were even less apposite and nobody was asked to tick any option which he did not believe to be approximately true. On this question too it was the political responses that were interesting – alas because they were up to one's worst caricatures of partisan attitudes. Nearly three-quarters of the Conservative sample remained unmoved by the implied tribute to market forces paid by Soviet bloc countries and gleefully ticked an answer which contained the clause 'socialism cannot work.' The majority of Labour M.P.s, on the other hand, were equally unattracted by the blandishments of a market economy based on state enterprise. Indeed, some 50 per cent rushed to endorse the statement that, even in a socialist economy 'the price of staples must be centrally controlled to avoid inflation.' The cause of any sort of market oriented social democracy has still made painfully little headway in the British Labour Party, even at the Parliamentary level.

There is another change of topic in Question 9. This contains the quotation: 'The bigger the volume the lower the cost; that is the first law of all industry.' A number of possible comments were provided. The 'correct' one read: 'Although true up to a point for virtually all products, the statement is inconsistent with a well-established finding of economics.' One can think of some somewhat pedantic senses in which this statement *must* be true if both extremely small and indefinitely large volumes are considered. Alternatively, the test compilers might have meant it as an empirical generalisation. Either way only about 40 per cent of the economists endorsed this particular 'right answer.'

The best way to interpret the responses to this ques-

tion is as a guide to how far people accepted the doc-
trines, especially fashionable in the 1960s, about the
great advantage of size and scale in industry. The
'correct' answer expressed a certain scepticism. So did
another alternative answer, that the original statement
about volume, 'although true for a limited number of
products ..., is not generally correct.' A third possible
answer which asserted that the statement embodied 'a
well-established generalisation applying to most products, but not to all of them,' came down on the side
of bigness. The fourth option provided was clearly
absurd, attracted hardly any support, and need not
detain us.

Only 40 per cent of the economists endorsed the
statement on the advantages of size alleged to prevail
for most products. Some 54 per cent ticked one of the
more sceptical comments and the remainder found the
question impossible to answer on the data provided.
By contrast nearly 80 per cent of Conservative M.P.s
and over 70 per cent of commentators accepted the
pro-size doctrine hook-line-and-sinker – just as if they
had just emerged from a high pressure course in the
Wedgwood Benn Mintech. Labour M.P.s also endorsed the pro-size point of view, but by a much
narrower majority. In this respect, their responses
resembled the business economists who, unlike other
economists, had a tendency to favour size – but less
overwhelmingly so than Tory politicians.

The only question in Section A which failed to reveal
any worthwhile information was the tenth one on the
Selective Employment Tax. It is, of course, a fallacy
to suppose that a general payroll tax, which would put
up the prices of machinery as well as labour would

promote labour-saving methods.[5] But, if a tax is imposed on one set of workers (in the service trades), this
can be expected to lead to a rise in labour productivity
there, as firms substitute other factors of production.
This way of putting things was accepted by 84 per cent
of the economists (with a distinctly higher percentage
among governmental than business economists). But
very little follows from it. Increasing labour productivity by subsidising machinery is not necessarily a
sensible objective for a particular sector, whatever one
may think of it for the economy as a whole. The whole
'efficiency' case for S.E.T. depends on an assumed difference in the readiness of employers to pass on higher
labour costs in services compared with employers in
manufacturing and/or on a view on the differential
productivity of workers transferred from services to
manufacturing (assuming that the transfer can be
made); the whole argument also needs to be related
to consumer preferences. The limited claim made in
the 'correct' answer does not by itself establish a case
for S.E.T., as several economists pointed out; and it
is not surprising that over half the Conservative M.P.s
could endorse it without wishing to question their
Party's intention of abolishing the whole tax.

10 'Would' and 'Should'

With Part B of the questionnaire we leave behind the
M.P.s and the commentators, and move to areas which
would be regarded as 'technical' by many politicians
and other educated laymen, and where considerable
indignation is expressed at the inability of economists
to agree in their findings. This section did, in fact,
unearth a fair amount of agreement – although no
more than in the apparently less technical and more
political Section A. Leaving out an omitted Question
in Section B, which turned out to be defective, the average percentage of economists agreeing with the
intended 'correct' answer was just over 75. Bearing in
mind the genuine ambiguities in the questions and the
tendency of some economists to find all questions impossible to answer in the terms stated, this is a high
degree of agreement.

But, although the replies showed an area of professional consensus on certain issues, such as demand
management, Budget deficits, monetary policy and
international currency, which are regarded as arcane
mysteries by the general public, this consensus was
established at the expense of ignoring vital areas of

dispute such as the diagnosis of and cure for wage–cost inflation, or the feasible minimum level of unemployment and how that could be lowered, to name but a few examples. Moreover, the economists outside the consensus who were sceptical of the ultimate influence of fiscal and monetary policy on real output and activity – whether they were neoclassical monetarists or ardent believers in physical intervention – cannot be dismissed by a pure counting of heads.

The most spirited debate was touched off by Question 1 of Part B, which listed four topics – the effects of joining the EEC, of reducing income tax and of devaluation, and whether fiscal policy *should* be used to distribute income more equally – and asked on which of these the economist could offer a personal opinion only and not a professional analysis. The correct answer was meant to be the last named topic. This followed from the use of the word 'should'. However inadequate the information or the economic model available for predicting the effects of, say, joining the EEC, this was in principle a professional exercise, while a view on the distribution of incomes involved a value judgement.

There was a considerable revolt against this orthodox view, which only 59 per cent of the economists in the sample accepted. About a fifth of the sample insisted that the effect of joining the EEC on real *per capita* income was a matter on which economists could only offer a personal opinion; and one-tenth stressed that some professional analysis was possible on *all* questions. These heretical standpoints were persuasively argued. Some economists for example stressed that all the questions involved both personal judgements and analysis; the element of personal judgement differed from one topic to another, but was one of degree rather than kind. Those who took this line may not have accepted the very special status attached to so-called 'value judgements', compared with other personal judgements, by the positivist school. Alternatively, they realised that it was not a simple matter to segregate value judgements from other assertions either in ordinary or technical language. Nearly all supposedly value judgements contain some implicit empirical assumptions, while most would-be factual assertions contain evaluative overtones.

Some respondents insisted, for example, that professional analysis was possible on the question about redistributive taxation. They did not, for the most part, expand on this and may have just meant that economists are concerned with whether redistributive taxation indeed has the egalitarian effects claimed for it. But they might also have meant something further. If such taxation were successful in securing something more nearly approaching an equal distribution of income, there would be certain effects on the character of society. There is room for professional analysis (whether one labels it economic or sociological) of what these effects would be; and it is perfectly reasonable to want to learn more about what these effects are likely to be, before deciding whether successful egalitarian policies 'should' or 'should not' be pursued, or to what extent.[6]

Question 2 of Part B provided a rare opportunity for a right-wing 'growth before redistribution' revolt. Four alternative comments were provided on the statement: 'Economic analysis has shown that to increase economic welfare any policy that would increase economic efficiency should always be undertaken.' The answer expected was that this was incorrect 'because an improved allocation of resources *can* increase everyone's real income, but *may* reduce someone's real income.' This was endorsed by over 78 per cent of the non-business economists. Two of the other possible answers were patently absurd on almost any professional definition of the terms in the opening statement and received virtually no support. The dissentients, who were especially prominent among the business economists (where the orthodox answer received only 57 per cent endorsement), either declared the question impossible to answer or, more frequently, ticked a fourth answer which read, 'Correct, because an improved allocation of resources *can* increase everyone's real income.'

One academic declared that the question was vague without explicitly bringing in the issue of actual or potential compensation to those who lost out from the change. But the question surely made it clear that compensation would not necessarily be paid. What the dissentients surely meant – and one or two of them were explicit about this – was that, as a general rule, measures to improve allocation should not be stopped out of an excessive preoccupation with distributional issues. Change, in their view, should only be prevented if there were a clear presumption that it would involve some undesirable shift in the distribution of income which was unlikely to be offset by compensatory action. This point of view slid over the portentous clause 'Economic analysis has shown'; but if the distributional approach had been followed in the past, one wonders if many of the economic advances that have occurred since Tudor times would have been permitted, and what the long-term effect of such a veto would have been on the standard of living of the poorest.

11 Unemployment

The third question of Part B plunged into the problems of why 'considerable unemployment can exist in a market economy.' The intended answer was: 'Many product and factor prices respond very slowly when supply exceeds demand.' The answer was supported in the *Interpretive Manual* with the statement that if 'prices and wages were completely flexible and responded quickly to situations of excess demand and excess supply, all markets, including the labour market, would clear. That is, full employment, apart from frictional elements, would always exist.' It was conceded that under certain extreme assumptions this reasoning might not be valid, but it was still the best of the available answers.

Here we came up against one of the snags in using examination questions for non-examination purposes. For, in order to make the other explanations demonstrably wrong, the Keynesian alternative was deliberately stated in the nonsensical form: 'At full employment national income is not always sufficient to purchase all output produced.' National income equals national output by definition (overseas investment

income apart); and many respondents suggested
amended phraseology, e.g. 'The level of real aggregate
demand (or expenditure) at full employment income
would not always be sufficient to purchase all the output produced.' Even so, only 58 per cent of the
respondents would accept the orthodox reply; and the
proportion fell below 50 per cent in the case of the
academics.

In this question there was a significant division
among governmental economists. Those concerned
with the Treasury, or central economic management,
voted in about the same proportion as the academics
while the remainder tended to side with the business economists in accepting the wage–price rigidity
explanation. Economists of a 'micro' bent evidently
thought in terms of individual markets writ large, while
the macro-economists realised that the problem was
more complicated for the economy as a whole, where
wage reduction was a reduction in demand as well as
costs, and any beneficial effect on employment would
have to come through a more complex roundabout
route.

Where economists amended the Keynesian explanation, before ticking it, or indicated that they would
have supported it if it had been phrased properly, they
have been labelled as endorsers in the table. But, even
with this adjustment, percentages shown in support of
the orthodox wage–price rigidity reply must be taken
as ceilings. Some 28 per cent of the academics either
found the question impossible to answer in the terms
stated or ticked more than one possible answer. There
must have been some respondents who ticked the
orthodox answer without comment mainly because of

the bad phrasing of the Keynesian alternative. Moreover, even among those who genuinely accepted the
orthodox price rigidity answer, several remarked that
it did not tell the whole story. It was clear too, that
most of the objections to, or reservations about, that
answer were not based on remote theoretical possibilities, such as the Keynesian 'liquidity trap', but on the
belief that it was not 'very illuminating' as a guide to
the real problems.

The whole idea of explanation in economics is
indeed very slippery. Two economists can be in complete agreement about the consequences of any specified wage–price behaviour or official financial policy;
but one of them, who takes downward wage rigidity
for granted, will regard the 'cause' of unemployment
as the failure of effective demand to keep pace with
supply, while another, who does not accept this rigidity,
can equally legitimately attribute unemployment to
the obstinacy of those who set wages in resistance to
market forces.

None of this need cause concern once understood.
More worrying was the sizeable minority of economists,
especially among the governmental group, who ticked,
as at least part of their explanation, the statement 'the
growth of productive capacity outstrips the growth of
consumers' private wants.' As the *Interpretive Manual*
points out, no nation has yet had sufficient resources
to be in the happy state of being able to satisfy all its
citizens' private wants; and it is sad that even a minority
of professionals concerned with central economic
management should have been so bemused by the
climb in unemployment towards the end of 1971, as
to accept the premature journalistic belief (expressed

in every recession) that economic satiety has already arrived. There is no such luck.

The fourth, fifth, sixth and seventh questions of Section B show that the much-discussed 'monetarist' critique of Keynesian economics has penetrated only skin-deep as far as the great majority of British economists are concerned. There is now some willingness to accept that monetary policy can have an important influence; but this is the most superficial aspect of monetarism, and, indeed, is fully consistent with Keynesian doctrine. The more extreme monetarist claim that fiscal policy has a negligible influence on the level of activity, except in so far as it involves change in the money supply, seems to have won very little acceptance. But the most fundamental of the monetarist claims as voiced by Friedman, which dwarfs all the others, is that demand management of any kind, whether by monetary or fiscal means, cannot have more than a temporary effect on the level of real output and employment and that the eventual effects of a boost to the money supply are entirely on the price level. This is a truly revolutionary – or counter-revolutionary – claim, which has received extraordinarily little acceptance or even attention in the British debate. The monetarists have largely themselves to blame for this because of their concentration on the monetary versus fiscal policy debate, and on short-term forecasting, rather than on these more fundamental matters.

This was brought out very clearly by Question 4, which had a long preamble purporting to depict a state of high employment verging on demand inflation, following a period of monetary and fiscal expansion. An (imaginary) 'leading economist' has proposed still further cuts in income tax or increases in government spending and the respondent is asked to choose an inference about his policy objectives. Some economists objected that the state of affairs envisaged was much too vaguely described to establish a conclusion. Even so, some 84 per cent accepted the orthodox inference, which was that the economist in question sought 'lower unemployment, even at the expense of a higher rate of inflation.'

An alternative Friedmanite answer might have run on the following lines. 'This economist may think that he will reduce unemployment still further; but this will not happen even for a temporary period unless the fiscal stimulus is financed by faster growth in the money supply. Even in that case the benefit to employment will eventually fade away and the long term effect will simply be a higher price level. If there is no change in the growth of the money supply, the effect of a larger Budget deficit will be a higher real rate of interest, more consumption and less investment – in other words, forced dissaving.' None of the alternative answers provided in the question was along these lines; and, although there was a certain amount of adverse comment on the question, hardly any respondent as much as hinted that he had a belief of this kind. The most outspoken remark from a British monetarist on the objectives of the economist who wished to cut taxes at a time of high demand was 'God knows!'

A completely different possibility suggested by a small, but articulate, minority was that the economist in question was a 'virtuous growthman,' who believed that a policy of sustained demand stimulation beyond the conventional limits would lead to the increase in the long term growth rate for so long sought in vain by British policy-makers. A more disillusioned variant of this thesis was that the economist was indeed a growthman, but mesmerised by a mistaken objective, while the most cynical comment of all was that he was secretly hoping for the collapse of the system.

Question 5 was based on an invented quotation from a Congressman who, speaking in circumstances of full employment and steady prices, advocated top priority to reducing the National Debt. This meant a Budget surplus year by year, reduced Federal spending and, if necessary, increased taxes. The respondent was asked whether, if this man had his way, the result would be increased unemployment and idle capacity, faster economic growth, both or neither, 'assuming other things remain the same.'

The replies showed a little more hesitation in writing off this Congressman as a backwoods simpleton than would have been the case a few years ago. Queries were raised about the time horizon. One economist said that it was self-contradictory to hold everything else the same in a general equilibrium system. Several asked what would happen to the debt repayments and declared the question impossible to answer without some information on the assumed behaviour of the money supply. Nevertheless, 89 per cent of the total and 95 per cent of governmental economists were prepared to tick 'increased unemployment and idle capacity only' as the nearest approximation to the truth. Only 1 per cent were prepared to tick faster growth and only 1 per cent were even prepared to subscribe to a mixture of the two effects. The latter seems to me the most plausible answer. This follows from (a) the attempts that the Federal Reserve or Bank of England would probably have made by the early 1970s (although not a decade previously) to ensure that the Budget surpluses did not prevent an adequate growth of the money supply and (b) the effects of the Congressman's policy on the investment : consumption ratio.

The following question, Number 6, attempted to paint a picture of demand inflation, with no unemployment problem, but with rapidly rising wages and prices. Some specific information on durable goods was also included to confuse the issue for the undergraduates for whom the question was originally intended. Four possible policies were suggested, of which the only suitable one was intended to be monetary restriction via an 'increase of reserve requirements of commercial banks.'

Support for the orthodox answer here was 77 per cent. One reason for the drop in size compared with the previous question was that two dud answers were given – *purchases* of securities by the central banks and the *lengthening* of the maximum instalment credit repayment period. It would have been very easy for an economist to misread 'purchase' and 'lengthening' for their opposites; and in a few cases this clearly happened. The tiny choir of those who wanted to push ahead regardless of inflation ('Why do anything') was again in evidence; and there were complaints that the policy goal was not specified. But the more important reason for the drop in the orthodox majority was a feeling that the one 'correct' response supplied, increased reserve requirements, was too feeble a weapon – occasionally because it was felt to be an inappropriate instrument of monetary restriction, but more often because of scepticism that monetary restraint could accomplish much. Even some of those who ticked it emphasised that it was 'not very good' and only the 'least inappropriate' of the list.

The 'wrong' answer that did attract a distinct minority of 13 per cent, either on its own or in combination with increased reserve requirements, was wholesale price ceilings. There was an obvious group of economists, who, throughout the enquiry, were looking for any respectable opportunity to knock the liberal orthodoxy, and the fact that Question 6 was not phrased so tightly as to exclude completely any element of cost inflation gave them an opportunity. Indeed, if the direct control advocated had been less crude than the wholesale price ceiling, it would almost certainly have attracted more support.

Question 7 yet again attempted to draw a picture of demand inflation, with greater emphasis on the very low level of unemployment. This time, however, the orthodox answer on offer was an increase in income tax. Again the percentage supporting it was 77; the dissentients were this time drawn from monetarist sympathisers. There was again a deliberately misleading reference to *purchases* of securities by the central bank, but on this occasion there was only a fiscalist 'correct' alternative for which to vote. The arguable heresy on offer this time was a pro-business one, lower taxes for corporations that increased investment, but it received only 6 per cent support even in conjunction with the increase in income tax. (The fourth option was a reference to more generous unemployment pay, which however desirable, was completely inappropriate as a remedy for demand inflation.)

The eighth question of Section B posed the problem of how to restrict aggregate private demand to prevent 'dramatic increases in expenditure for the war abroad' from causing serious inflation. Respondents were asked whether higher interest rates or higher personal income tax would have 'the lesser adverse effect' on economic growth. Here the support for the orthodox answer of an increase in personal income taxes rose to 84 per cent. There were the usual purist complaints about an incompletely specified question. More interesting were those who said that the increase in income tax was the correct answer, but confessed that their confidence in it had waned over the last few years, or even that they had instinctive misgivings. Only 3 per cent were prepared to accept the robust 'wrong' answer that each policy would have 'the same effect on economic growth – that is, no effect, because economic growth is independent of governmental action.' There were, however, remarks indicating that the percentage favouring this answer would have been higher if the words 'no effect' had been omitted.

The most impressive result was the overwhelming majority for the orthodox answer among governmental economists whenever that answer pointed to an increase in income tax – 97 per cent in this question and 89 per cent in the previous one. There was no suggestion here of a bolt towards heresy; and the supposedly favourable distributional implications no doubt added a particular sweetener to the anti-inflationary virtue.

The ninth and final question of Part B listed four possible arguments for 'an increase in the world's supply of international monetary reserves by creating a new international currency ("paper gold").' The question did not seem to excite enthusiasm or provoke a great deal of illuminating comment. The intended answer was: 'The demand for gold and reserve currencies is growing faster than supply.' This received 78 per cent support. The other answers were clearly inappropriate to the question, and those who did not accept the orthodox answer tended to say that none of the alternatives gave an adequate argument. A few pointed out that the envisaged situation was also an argument for an increase in the official price of gold. One governmental economist stressed that the problem was the *quality* rather than the quantity of international reserve assets.

The most interesting revelation had nothing to do with international reserves, but with the different attitudes to language and concepts of economists with identical views on the need for 'paper gold.' There were distinguished authorities who were quite happy with the wording of the question and intended answer as brief accounts of the problem, while others regarded it as grossly inadequate and even raged at the alleged meaninglessness of the 'demand for' and 'supply of' reserves. This made one sympathise with some of the student critiques of the validity and reliability of examinations, whether of the orthodox essay, or multiple choice, type. Of course, an intelligent student can devote attention to the foibles and preferences of those likely to examine him as well as to the subject itself; and anyone who has had to submit articles for publication has had to engage in a similar exercise. Yet, I doubt if this is a wholly admirable activity or whether one should regard as inferior those who have a distaste for this particular brand of lifemanship.

12 Concluding Thoughts

The degree of agreement among economists, assessed by the average percentage accepting the intended answer, was almost identical in Sections A and B. Yet, in many ways, the extent of agreement in Section A was as remarkable as the degree of disagreement in Section B. The first section covered politically charged, highly controversial topics; yet economists achieved a substantial degree of consensus, which set them apart from both Labour and Conservative politicians – who on most topics had more in common with each other than either group had with the economists. On the other hand, the second Section dealt with objectives such as employment, growth, containing inflation, and international monetary stability, on which there is an apparently strong political consensus and a readiness to follow professional opinion if it would only point the way.

Yet such economic consensus as was achieved here was faced by a dissenting minority of some intellectual respectability, every bit as large as on the more obviously political questions; and it was, moreover, achieved only by leaving aside an enormous area of relevant controversy. The questionnaire only just touched the question whether a much higher level of demand (with or without an 'incomes policy') would lead to a virtuous circle of growth and lower prices, growth alone, or simply to an explosive and unsustainable inflation culminating in 'go–stop,' and less growth rather than more. One can find learned pieces of econometrics to justify all these incompatible positions.

On two consecutive days in October 1971 *The Financial Times* published letters from one of the leading younger monetary economists at the L.S.E. and one of the best known members of the N.I.E.S.R. staff. Both were commenting on articles that had appeared on the prevailing unemployment problem. The first letter urged the need to distinguish between (a) the unemployable, (b) those voluntarily changing jobs, (c) those not prepared to move to different districts or types of jobs and (d) those involuntarily unemployed, though they were prepared to move. Until the size of the fourth category was isolated, the writer suggested, it was intellectually dishonest to beat the 'reflationary' drum. The second letter disclaimed any need for such distinctions, remarking that 'with a generally high pressure of demand,' the people in the first three categories always find a niche and are unemployable no longer. The argument ultimately turns, not just on different social values, but also on different views of the feasibility and consequences of running the economy at a consistently 'higher pressure of demand.' If the argument were pursued further there would be differences not merely on the risks of an inflationary explosion bringing the experiment to an end, but also on the advisability of policies of a non-financial kind (i.e. incomes policies) for tackling such dangers if they did emerge; and these differences in turn would involve different views both of the probable success of such policies and of their desirability. It is sheer wishful thinking that such complex sources of disagreement are likely to be sorted out quickly, if at all.

Technical economics has indeed remarkably little to say about the causes of the 'Wealth of Nations' – and therefore of the long-term effects of joining the EEC. At an anniversary dinner of the Political Economy Club, Lord Robbins demonstrated that many contemporary arguments were already current in the early 19th century, and it is a myth to assume that they will be quickly resolved – any more by the importation of sociology today than by the importation of techniques from the physical sciences, from which so much was hoped in the 1930s.

As can be readily imagined, I received a number of interesting little essays from correspondents on the nature of disagreement in economics. One university teacher remarked that much public impatience with disagreement among economists on apparently factual questions was the result of misunderstanding of the nature of the subject of 'an analytical discipline.' This could 'only indicate the conditions under which certain propositions are true and predictions follow.' He believed, for instance, that if, instead of asking economists whether EEC entry would accelerate growth, they were instead asked 'Under what conditions would the U.K. growth rate accelerate on entry to the EEC?', there would be much less disagreement. There were some perfectly feasible reactions within the U.K. after entry that would, if they transpired, turn the most ardent

EEC advocates against membership. Similarly there were other possible reactions 'which would make serious anti-marketeers more favourably inclined to membership.' (The latter is perhaps a fond hope.)

There are, indeed, a good many more limited issues on which economists could, if they went in a little less for product differentiation, offer useful advice which would carry a high degree of professional consensus. For example, many of both the 'pro' and the 'anti' EEC economists would agree on the implications of the so-called Werner Plan for monetary union or of the Common Agricultural Policy. It is easy enough to state the ideal qualities which should be exhibited in public pronouncements by an economist. He should first emphasise the areas and topics on which there is some consensus and then go on to the areas of disagreement, explaining as far as possible how far these are about cause-and-effect relationships and how far they involve differing judgements about the goals for which we should aim. He should also attempt to highlight some of the more subtle differences in conceptual frameworks or ways of seeing the world which cannot, without further analysis, be easily fitted into the fact–value dichotomy. At the end of such an exposition he might then tentatively offer his own contribution to the unresolved issues.

Yet there are deep-seated reasons why such procedures are rarely followed, apart from their difficulty and tedium. The frequent charge of political bias is usually put in the wrong form. Where the work of an economist leads him to certain political conclusions he has every right and even duty to promulgate them. Nor should he be deterred by fear of introducing value judgements provided he is frank about them. Many apparent value judgements are, as already discussed, susceptible to further analysis. The undesirable kind of political bias is different. It is where economists make partisan points designed to provide respectable ammunition for the political party they favour – sometimes in opposition to their own basic beliefs. This was particularly noticeable in the U.S. in 1971, where some pro-Republican economists defended the Nixon wage and price controls, while Democrat economists searched around for niggling points of criticism – despite the fact that Mr Nixon probably moved much further in their direction than a Democratic President would have dared in his place.

Some economists steer admirably clear of anything resembling partisan debating points but succumb to a lure of a different sort. They are tempted to fall in with the latest fashion and to advocate, for instance, incomes policies or the replacement of reserve currencies by paper units. But there is also a sophisticated market for those who are prepared deliberately to go against fashion and deride what they believe to be the conventional wisdom. Unfortunately, economists of this latter brand are apt to change their opinions with such rapidity that any layman who tries to base himself on their pronouncements would soon feel bewildered and shellshocked. Indeed, one is often struck by the way in which the severest academic critics of the journalistic approach outdo all the journalists in their desire for novelty and effect.

If we are to understand these various bad habits, it is necessary to examine the market for economists' pronouncements. A profession that spends so much time examining other people's markets might profitably devote a little time to examining its own. Like other producers, economists prosper by studying the market and supplying what it appears to want.

Both at the academic level and at that of public pronouncements, prizes are to be won by product differentiation. There is little doubt that leading economists can make a notable, if superficial, impact by making their pronouncements appear as different as possible from those of their colleagues, and by putting the emphasis on those points which they believe to be original rather than on the common elements on which most economists agree. This was illustrated by a cocktail party in Washington where one economist present remarked: 'I have got some really smashing evidence to present to Congress tomorrow,' but refused to disclose its nature in case he was pre-empted by someone else. There is, in fact, a deep-seated ambivalence in public attitudes towards economists. While people delight in ridiculing them for their disagreements, they are also entertained by original, provocative and controversial viewpoints; and a high price and some prestige can be gained by meeting this public demand. The key to understanding many economic pronouncements is that they belong at least as much to the entertainment as the information industry.

It would be misleading to suppose that market considerations are absent at the purely academic level. The main market here is, of course, for learned papers. The contribution of such papers to economic understanding is one criterion by which they are judged. But it is not the only one, and it is a very elusive and intangible quality to assess. More important in practice tends to be 'professional competence.' This is something rather different, involving the sophistication of the statistical and mathematical methods used, knowledge of, and references to, the previous literature, internal consistency and so on. It is much more important for a paper to be competent than for it to be right or enlightening. The prizes are to be gained by slightly differentiating one's theories and methods from those of other economists, while staying within the general professional canons mentioned above.

Another aspect of the contemporary economic scene is the stress on quantification and prediction. Indeed, Professor Harry Johnson claims that ability here 'now constitutes the economists' main claim to superiority as a profession over the general run of intelligent men with an interest in economic problems.' (His views are to be found in *Australian Economic Papers*, June, 1971.) A dissenting opinion is, however, provided by Professor Hayek who remarks that 'what we must get rid of is the naïve superstition that the world must be so organised that it is possible by direct observation to discover simple regularities between all phenomena and that this is a necessary presupposition for the application of scientific method' (*Studies in Philosophy, Politics and Economics*). Hayek's view is that economics enables one to predict certain general features of a situation, but not particular consequences.

One does not need to go quite so far. Specific predictions are useful when they can be obtained. But even if they cannot be, some good generalisations are a good deal better than nothing. Indeed, the most important advice that needs to be given often involves extremely elementary economics which, in the words of one of the respondents to the questionnaire, it takes a lifetime of experience to apply.

But wherever the right balance lies in this argument, it is hard to imagine the academic market being any different. When economists consisted of a small band of gentlemen scholars, as they did in the age of David Hume, Adam Smith and Ricardo (and to a lesser extent up to the eve of the Second World War), it was possible to put great weight on general insight, and to allow room for a variety of methods and approaches. With the explosive growth of the profession since the end of the war, and the need to fill hundreds of new teaching posts, an emphasis on technical competence in the narrow sense was probably the only way of keeping any sort of watch on standards; indeed, British economists have still to work out of their system a partially justified inferiority complex in relation to American professional techniques.

Similar considerations apply to economists in Whitehall, especially in the central policy-making departments such as the Treasury. If official advice concentrated on applying elementary home truths and on frank discussion of underlying issues, the need for employing large numbers of specialist advisers might be called into question. On the other hand, economic forecasting looks like a highly technical service which Permanent Secretaries could hardly provide for themselves with the aid of a scribbling pad. No matter how often forecasts can go wrong, the moral that is drawn is that one should continue to work to improve them.

The really interesting tensions in economics do not, however, lie in these make-work devices, but in the unresolved question whether the subject is concerned with the production and expansion of material wealth, or whether it is concerned with the logic of choice in which no particular priority is given to any end. Another fascinating question is the intimate relationship between economics as a would-be science and what I have termed the liberal-orthodox ideology. There are deep-seated reasons for this connection (which I have discussed in *Capitalism and the Permissive Society*, pp. 144 et seq.), and which will not be easily broken by incantations about value-free economics.

But however unresolved the debate on these perennial issues, and however short of scientific proof one is on some of the larger questions of cause-and-effect, this does not mean that the subject is nonsense. The fact that philosophers still disagree over age-old topics, such as determinism or free will, does not mean that anyone's opinion on these topics is as good as anyone else's or that there are not different levels of debating them; and the same applies to political economy.

Notes and References

1. As Appendix 2 to 'University Students' Initial Understanding of Economics: The Contribution of "A" Level Economics Course and Other Factors' by Richard Attiyeh and Keith G. Lumsden.

2. See K. G. Lumsden (ed.), *Recent Research in Economic Education* (Prentice-Hall, 1970).

3. *Interpretive Manual for the T.E.C. – Advanced Level* (Esmée Fairbairn Economics Research Centre, 1971).

4. *Journalists at Work* (Constable, 1971), pp. 171–3.

5. This is explained very clearly in E. J. Mishan, *21 Popular Economic Fallacies* (Allen Lane, 1969), Chapter 2.

6. This view is persuasively argued by F. A. Hayek in 'The Economy, Science and Politics', reprinted in *Studies in Philosophy, Politics and Economics* (Routledge & Kegan Paul, 1967), pp. 258–9.

Appendixes

1 Letter to Economists

I should like to ask your co-operation on a small project on which I am engaged. The object is to investigate the degree of agreement which exists among economists on certain basic questions of interest to a wider public. For this special purpose, I have put together a multiple choice questionnaire of items originally intended for undergraduates. These are compiled from various 'tests of economics comprehension' devised by the Economics Education Project in the U.K. and the U.S. Joint Council on Economic Education. You will, of course, understand that I am in no way seeking to 'test' economists, but rather to see how much agreement there is among them on the correct answers.

I should therefore be extremely grateful if you could spare a little while to read through the questions and tick the answers you regard as appropriate. You will notice that the questionnaire has been divided into two parts. The first, some of which may seem fairly elementary, covers fairly general questions frequently discussed by non-economists. The second part ventures more into the macro-economic and monetary realms. All answers will be treated as entirely confidential. I may want to include in any published work a list of those who have taken part; but I shall, of course, omit your name if you ask me to do so.

If you feel strongly that any of the questions is too badly phrased to answer, please feel free to say this. But can you please give the test the benefit of the doubt and tick any answer which you think is a reasonable approximation to the truth from the point of view of a student or member of the general public. I should be extremely grateful if you could find enough time to study the questions so that answers different from the standard ones would indicate genuine disagreement with the compilers of the test.

If you have yourself been *very extensively* involved in administering the tests, please do not bother to reply, as I am seeking responses from those to whom the questions are reasonably fresh, although not necessarily entirely novel.

Do please excuse me for taking up your time. My only excuse is that you too may find the results of this investigation of some interest.

Yours sincerely,

Samuel Brittan

2 Letter to Politicians and Commentators

PRIVATE AND CONFIDENTIAL

I should like to ask for your co-operation on a small project on which I am engaged. The object is to find out the degree of consensus or disagreement that exists among leading political figures on certain key economic questions. I should therefore be extremely grateful if you could spare a little while to read through the enclosed questionnaire and tick the answers you regard as appropriate. I give you my personal word that *all answers and the identity of those taking part will be treated as entirely confidential.*

The questionnaire has already been sent to a number of economists, with extremely interesting results. I am now sending it to a selected group of M.P.s and political commentators for purposes of comparison. Although the items have been selected from multiple choice questionnaires originally designed for students,* you will see that I have selected those with direct relevance to

* Compiled from various 'tests of economics comprehension' devised by the Economics Education Project in the U.K. and the U.S. Joint Council on Economic Education.

public policy. There is, of course, no question of 'testing' any of the recipients of this present enquiry. The whole object is to see how much agreement or disagreement there is among them on the answers.

If you feel strongly that any of the questions is too badly phrased to answer, please feel free to say this. But can you please give the test the benefit of the doubt and tick any answer which you think is a reasonable approximation to the truth.

Do please forgive me for taking up your time. My only excuse is that you too may find the results of this investigation of some interest.

Yours sincerely,

Samuel Brittan

3 Questionnaire and Replies

The original text of the questionnaire is in Roman type. Additional categories subsequently added, or further explanatory wording to help in tabulation, are in italics. For the convenience of the reader, the order of the provided alternative answers in some of the questions has been changed. The original order can be easily seen from their letter headings. The figures in the columns are in percentages. The number of replies in each particular category is shown in brackets at the top of the column.

PART A

QUESTION 1

In order to make the most efficient use of a city's resources, how should tube and bus fares vary during the day?

	'Correct' Answer	Academic Economists (44) %	Governmental Economists (37) %	Business Economists (21) %	TOTAL ECONOMISTS† (117) %	Conservative M.P.s (39) %	Labour M.P.s (52) %	Commentators (24) %
(b) They should be relatively low during rush hour to transport as many people as possible at that time.		—	—	—	1	—	21	17
(a) They should be relatively low during rush hour to reduce costs for the maximum number of people. *(Including those giving both (a) and (b).)*		—	3	—	1	—	19	8
(d) They should be the same at all times to avoid making travellers alter their schedules because of price differences.		—	5	10	4	60	39	42
(c) They should be relatively high during rush hour to minimise the amount of equipment needed to transport the daily travellers.	*	91	84	90	88	35	19	25
Impossible to answer on the data and alternatives given.		9	8	—	6	5	2	8

† Includes 15 economists answering anonymously whose category could not be traced.

Questions 2 and 3 are based on the following information:

Smog in the Central City area is largely caused by automobile exhaust fumes. The smog problem could be virtually eliminated if approximately 100 air-purification plants were built in the area. These plants would simply draw in smog-filled air, remove the smog, and pump the clean air back into the Central City atmosphere. It is estimated that the cost of operating each plant would be £25,000 per year.

QUESTION 2

It is highly unlikely that private business firms would build and operate the plants and sell their services directly to individual residents of the Central City area because:

	'Correct' Answer	Academic Economists	Governmental Economists	Business Economists	TOTAL ECONOMISTS	Conservative M.P.s	Labour M.P.s	Commentators
(a) The cost of operating the plants would be too great.		—	3	—	1	—	10	4
(b) People are unlikely to be willing to pay for smog-free air.		9	5	24	11	22	4	17
(c) It would be less costly for the government to build and operate the plants than for private business firms to do so.		—	—	—	—	—	17	21
(d) It would be impossible to provide smog-free air to those who are willing to pay for it while withholding it from those who refuse to pay.	*	82	92	62	82	43	48	37
Those giving (d) plus one or more other reasons.		9	—	14	6	22	17	8
Impossible to answer . . .		—	—	—	—	13	4	13

QUESTION 3

Suppose that the government of the Central City were to build and operate the air-purification plants. From the standpoint of achieving efficiency in the allocation of economic resources, which of the following taxes should be increased to provide the additional tax revenues needed to finance the operation of the air-purification plants?

	'Correct' Answer	Academic Economists	Governmental Economists	Business Economists	TOTAL ECONOMISTS	Conservative M.P.s	Labour M.P.s	Commentators
(b) General sales		—	5	5	3	19	4	17
(c) Property		7	5	9	11	11	9	13
(d) Income		2	13	—	5	8	29	8
(a) Motor vehicle fuel	*	77	69	81	71	43	42	58
Those giving motor vehicle and/or one other tax		2	5	5	4	3	8	4
Other combinations		—	—	—	—	—	3	—
Impossible to answer		12	3	—	6	16	2	—

QUESTION 4

As compared to a direct social security payment, how would you evaluate the provision of below-cost public housing to poor persons from the point of view of satisfying consumers' wants?

	'Correct' Answer	Academic Economists	Governmental Economists	Business Economists	TOTAL ECONOMISTS	Conservative M.P.s	Labour M.P.s	Commentators
(a) It is more efficient because it gives low income persons what they need.		23	19	19	22	30	69	63
(c) It is more efficient because it cannot be spent on undesirable goods such as tobacco and drink. (*Or both (a) and (c)*.)		5	—	33	9	8	11	8
(d) It is less efficient because the government cannot manage housing efficiently		—	5	10	4	22	2	17
(b) It is less efficient because it will result in too much housing and too little of the other things consumers want. (*Or for other reasons, apart from (d), in the case of M.P.s and commentators.*)	*	52	66	38	51	27	10	8
Both (b) and (d).		2	5	—	3	5	—	—
Impossible to answer		18	5	5	11	8	8	4

QUESTION 5

The most important economic function of rental payments for the use of land is to:

(c) Equalise the distribution of factor payments.
(a) Assure owners of land some return on its use.
(d) Assure an adequate supply of land in the society as a whole.
(b) Influence how land will be used. (*Or any combination including (b) in case of M.P.s and commentators.*)
Other combinations.
Impossible to answer . . .

	'Correct' Answer	Academic Economists	Governmental Economists	Business Economists	TOTAL ECONOMISTS	Conservative M.P.s	Labour M.P.s	Commentators
(c)		2	3	—	2	—	2	4
(a)		—	—	—	—	35	31	33
(d)		—	11	14	7	22	27	17
(b)	*	96	83	86	89	32	36	42
Other combinations.		—	—	—	—	3	—	—
Impossible to answer . . .		2	3	—	2	8	4	4

QUESTION 6

Which, if any, of the following statements would be correct when applied to a private enterprise economy?

(a) One of the principal effects of competition is to force prices to the lowest level consistent with normal prices.
(b) One of the principal functions of profits is to indicate to the government where wages are too low.

i) (a) only
ii) (b) only
iii) both (a) and (b)
iv) neither (a) nor (b)

	'Correct' Answer	Academic Economists	Governmental Economists	Business Economists	TOTAL ECONOMISTS	Conservative M.P.s	Labour M.P.s	Commentators
i) (a) only	*	84	89	81	83	87	42	67
ii) (b) only		—	—	—	—	—	—	—
iii) both (a) and (b)		—	—	5	1	—	2	8
iv) neither (a) nor (b)		16	11	14	16	13	56	25

QUESTION 7

In a free-enterprise economy, the presumed harmony between individual and public interest depends upon:

	'Correct' Answer	Academic Economists	Governmental Economists	Business Economists	TOTAL ECONOMISTS	Conservative M.P.s	Labour M.P.s	Commentators
(b) Careful planning and co-ordination of economic activity.		2	3	14	5	14	31	42
(c) The exercise of social responsibility by private businessmen.		2	5	10	6	14	23	12
Both (b) and (c).		2	—	5	2	—	8	4
(a) A strong desire for profit maximisation.		2	3	5	3	14	4	17
(d) Competitive markets and pursuit of self-interest by individuals.	*	78	84	57	74	35	17	17
Both (a) and (d).		2	—	—	2	10	6	—
Other mixtures.		2	5	9	5	8	2	8
Impossible to answer ...		10	—	—	3	5	9	—

Question 8 is based on the following quotation:

'The programme of economic reform shatters the rigidity of central planning, establishes realistic prices and eliminates subsidies. It forces each factory to pay its own way or close down. There was no other way but to start using the market again. If we take free enterprise to mean free price competition in the market, then even socialism cannot do without this enterprise. Only a few staples will have centrally-fixed prices. All others will be allowed to move freely in response to supply and demand.'

QUESTION 8

This report of changes taking place in many of the Soviet bloc countries supports the view of many Western economists that:

	'Correct' Answer	Academic Economists	Governmental Economists	Business Economists	TOTAL ECONOMISTS	Conservative M.P.s	Labour M.P.s	Commentators
(a) Even when a socialist economy relies on supply and demand to set most prices, the prices of staples must be centrally controlled to avoid inflation.		7	—	14	7	—	56	13
(b) A freely-operating market system can perform efficiently the function of allocating scarce resources to satisfy competing wants under socialism as well as under capitalism. (*Subsidiary reasons occasionally added by M.P.s and commentators.*)	*	77	84	67	77	21	21	50
(c) Socialism cannot work because it requires rigid central planning and and unrealistic prices which cannot allocate resources efficiently. (*Subsidiary reasons occasionally added by M.P.s and commentators.*)		2	8	14	8	73	2	33
(d) A free enterprise system is essentially the same as socialism.		2	3	5	2	3	6	4
Impossible to answer ...		12	5	—	6	3	15	—

	'Correct' Answer	Academic Economists	Governmental Economists	Business Economists	TOTAL ECONOMISTS	Conservative M.P.s	Labour M.P.s	Commentators
(a) The quotation correctly states one of the laws of economics.		—	—	—	—	3	2	4
(b) Although not a scientific law, the statement embodies a well established generalisation applying to most products, but not to all of them.		43	32	57	40	76	50	67
(c) Although true for a limited number of products, the statement is not generally correct.		9	19	10	14	8	13	4
(d) Although true up to a point for virtually all products, the statement is inconsistent with a well-established finding of economics.	*	39	46	33	40	13	29	17
Impossible to answer		9	3	—	6	—	6	8

QUESTION 9

'The bigger the volume, the lower the cost; that is the first law of all industry.' Which of the following best describes this quotation?

QUESTION 10

'The Selective Employment Tax (SET) in effect requires a non-manufacturing firm to pay a tax for each worker it employs. For these firms the SET can be expected, in the long run, to lead to an increase in output per worker.'

Is this statement correct or incorrect and why?

	'Correct' Answer	Academic Economists	Governmental Economists	Business Economists	TOTAL ECONOMISTS	Conservative M.P.s	Labour M.P.s	Commentators
(a) Correct, because the SET will increase efficiency. (*Including both (a) and (b)*.)		7	8	5	6	5	27	4
(b) Correct, because a rise in labour productivity can be expected in the long run when firms substitute other factors of production for labour.	*	75	92	86	84	49	59	63
(c) Incorrect, because the SET will decrease efficiency. (*Including both (c) and (d)*.)		4	—	—	2	11	2	8
(d) Incorrect, because a decline in labour productivity can be expected in the long run when firms contract output and employment.		—	—	—	1	22	6	21
Impossible to answer . . .		14	—	9	7	13	6	4

PART B

QUESTION 1

On which of the following can an economist offer only a personal opinion, not professional analysis?

	'Correct' Answer	Academic Economists	Governmental Economists	Business Economists	TOTAL
(a) Whether real income *per capita* in Britain would rise if Britain joined the Common Market.		9	8	—	6
(b) Whether taxes should be changed to distribute income more evenly.	*	65	67	48	59
(c) Whether a decrease in income tax would lead to higher national income.		—	5	5	3
(d) Whether devaluation of the pound would improve the British balance of payments.		—	—	—	—
Those mentioning combinations of issues including (a) and (b).		9	6	9	13
Other combinations.		2	8	19	7
None, i.e. professional analysis possible on all.		15	6	19	10
Impossible to answer on the data and alternatives given.		—	—	—	2

QUESTION 2

Is the following statement correct or incorrect and why?

'Economic analysis has shown that to increase economic welfare any policy that would increase economic efficiency should always be undertaken.'

	'Correct' Answer	Academic Economists	Governmental Economists	Business Economists	TOTAL
(a) Correct, because an improved allocation of resources *will* increase everyone's real income.		2	3	—	4
(b) Correct, because an improved allocation of resources *can* increase everyone's real income.		12	11	38	16
(c) Incorrect, because an improved allocation of resources *can* increase everyone's real income, but *may* reduce someone's real income.	*	79	78	57	74
(d) Incorrect, because an improved allocation of resources *cannot* increase everyone's real income.		—	3	5	2
Impossible to answer ...		7	5	—	4

QUESTION 3

Which of the following explains why considerable unemployment can exist in a market economy?

	'Correct' Answer	Academic Economists	Governmental Economists	Business Economists	TOTAL
(a) At full employment national income is not always sufficient to purchase all output produced.		21	17	10	16
(b) Many product and factor prices respond very slowly when supply exceeds demand.	*	47	55	71	58
(c) The rate of productivity increase is not always great enough to keep interest rates low.		—	—	—	—
(d) The growth of productive capacity outstrips the growth of consumers' private wants.		4	14	10	8
More than one answer given (invariably including (a) or (b)).		14	—	—	6
None adequate.		14	14	9	12

QUESTION 4

In response to expansionary monetary and fiscal policy national income has risen to an all time high, unemployment has fallen to its lowest level in three years, and the rate of inflation, though somewhat higher than in recent years, is only slightly above the historical average. A leading economist has proposed that for the coming year the government reduce income taxes or increase its spending.

What can be inferred about the economist's policy objectives? He seeks:

	'Correct' Answer	Academic Economists	Governmental Economists	Business Economists	TOTAL
(a) Lower unemployment, even at the expense of a higher rate of inflation.	*	84	89	67	84
(b) A lower rate of inflation, even at the expense of higher unemployment.		—	—	...	—
(c) Lower unemployment and lower interest rates.		—	3	28	7
(d) None of the above. (Or impossible to answer . . .)		16	8	5	9

	'Correct' Answer	Academic Economists	Governmental Economists	Business Economists	TOTAL

Question 5 is based on the following quotation:

'I have pledged myself to my constituents to do everything in my power to reduce the Federal Government's debt. This means a budget surplus every year until our goal has been reached. It means reducing Federal expenditure and, if necessary, increasing tax rates. Under present circumstances of full employment and steady prices, we can afford to bear the burden of debt ourselves instead of passing the burden on to our children and grandchildren.'

QUESTION 5

If the expressed wishes of the Congressman quoted were attained, what changes could be expected in the future (assuming other things remain the same)?

Key: i) Increased unemployment and idle capacity.
ii) Increased rates of economic growth.

	'Correct' Answer	Academic Economists	Governmental Economists	Business Economists	TOTAL
(a) i) only.	*	84	95	95	89
(b) ii) only.		—	—	—	1
(c) Both i) and ii).		—	—	5	1
(d) Neither i) nor ii). (*Or impossible to answer* . . .)		16	5	—	9

QUESTION 6

'Unit sales of durable goods last month were unprecedented. Recent price rises have lifted indexes towards the highest level of the century. Average wholesale price increases have been in excess of 1% a month during the past year. Unit wage costs, as a result of soaring wage rates without equal gains in productivity, are 5% higher for durable goods now than in the third quarter of last year, and 4% higher for non-durable goods. Unemployment is not a real problem at this time.'

Which of the following policies would be most appropriate?

	'Correct' Answer	Academic Economists	Governmental Economists	Business Economists	TOTAL
(a) Imposing of price ceilings on sales made by wholesale establishments.	*	7	8	19	10
(b) Increase of the reserve requirements of commercial banks.		73	87	62	77
Mention of (a) and/or (b).		7	—	5	3
(c) Purchase of securities by the central banks.		2	5	9	5
(d) Lengthening of the maximum repayment period on instalment credit for purchases of consumer goods.		11	—	5	5
Impossible to answer . . .					

QUESTION 7

'Last month new highs were reached both in industrial employment and industrial wages. Unemployment is at its lowest mark since World War II. In the week just ended, steel production reached the highest mark in history. The latest reported increase in the cost of living, with prices up 1·4% per month, was slightly higher than the average increase for the past eight months.'

Which of the following policies would be the most appropriate?

	'Correct' Answer	Academic Economists	Governmental Economists	Business Economists	TOTAL
(c) An across-the-board increase in personal income tax.	*	75	89	67	77
(a) Lower taxes for corporations that increase investment.		2	3	9	3
Both (a) and (c).		2	—	5	3
(b) Purchase of securities by the central bank.		5	5	19	7
(d) Increase of the maximum period unemployed workers may draw unemployment compensation.		5	—	—	5
None. (Or impossible to answer . . .)		11	3	—	5

QUESTION 8

Dramatic increases in expenditure for the war abroad are likely to cause serious inflation at home unless the government restricts the growth of aggregate private demand. Currently the government is considering either increasing interest rates or increasing personal income taxes. Which policy would have the lesser adverse effect on economic growth?

	'Correct' Answer	Academic Economists	Governmental Economists	Business Economists	TOTAL
(a) The increase in interest rates, because this will restrict consumption expenditures more than investment expenditure.		5	—	10	3
(b) The increase in interest rates, because this will restrict investment expenditure more than consumption expenditure.		5	—	10	3
(c) The increase in personal income taxes, because this will restrict consumption expenditure more than investment expenditure.	*	79	97	66	84
(d) Each policy will have the same effect on economic growth; that is, no effect, because economic growth is independent of government actions.		2	—	—	3
Impossible to answer ...		9	3	14	7

QUESTION 9

Which of the following is a valid argument supporting an increase in the world's supply of international monetary reserves by creating a new international currency ('paper gold')?

	'Correct' Answer	Academic Economists	Governmental Economists	Business Economists	TOTAL
(a) The demand for gold and reserve currencies is growing faster than supply.	*	79	81	76	78
(b) An increase in the dollar price of gold would not add to the world's monetary reserves but would only help gold-producing countries.		—	3	—	2
(c) Large deficits in the U.S. balance of payments with key countries are likely to continue for some time and have been draining the world of its supply of international monetary reserves.		—	3	5	2
(d) International agencies such as the World Bank and the International Monetary Fund hold large amounts of gold and convertible currencies and thus have reduced the available quantity of international reserves.		2	—	5	2
Those giving combinations of above.		7	—	—	4
None adequate. (Or impossible to answer . . .)		12	13	14	12

Source of Questions: A.1, A.4, A.10, B.4, B.8, B.9—Test of Economics Comprehension, *Economica*, February, 1971. A.6, B.1, B.2, B.3—Test of Economics Comprehension, *Economics Education Project, Paper II,* Esmée Fairbairn Economics Research Centre, Edinburgh. A.2, A.3, A.5, A.7, A.8, A.9, B.5, B.6, B.7—U.S. Test of Understanding in College Economics.

The category 'Impossible to answer on the data and alternatives given', in Questions A.4, A.5, and A.7, includes a few M.P.s and commentators who said they did not understand the question.

The column 'academic economists' contains six anonymous entries traced geographically by their postmark with a very high degree of confidence. 'Governmental economists' contain four originally anonymous entries which were traced to Whitehall with a reasonable degree of confidence. There remained fifteen untraceable anonymous entries.

4 Economists Taking Part

The list below excludes all economists in Government Departments, the Bank of England and the National Economic Development Office. It also excludes a few other economists who did not wish to have their names mentioned, as well, of course, as all those who replied anonymously.

Name	*Academic Institution*
R. Shaw	Aberdeen
A. R. Ilersic	Bedford
J. R. C. Lecomber	Bristol
P. M. Deane	Cambridge
W. A. H. Godley	Cambridge
C. D. Harbury	City University
I. Buchanan	Dundee
J. van Doorn	Durham
C. Bliss	Essex
R. L. Smyth	Keele
A. I. Macbean	Lancaster
E. Brunner	Lancaster
G. H. Peters	Liverpool
R. Alford	London School of Economics and Political Science
A. C. L. Day	London School of Economics and Political Science
T. Josling	London School of Economics and Political Science
A. A. Walters	London School of Economics and Political Science

Name	*Academic Institution*
M. C. Kennedy	Manchester
D. E. W. Laidler	Manchester
F. Blackaby	National Institute of Economic and Social Research
C. A. Blyth	National Institute of Economic and Social Research
M. Gregory	National Institute of Economic and Social Research
R. L. Major	National Institute of Economic and Social Research
I. Smith	Newcastle upon Tyne
N. J. Gibson	New University of Ulster
D. S. Lees	Nottingham
D. T. Llewellyn	Nottingham
F. S. Brooman	Open University
R. Thomas	Open University
A. D. Hazlewood	Oxford
I. M. D. Little	Oxford
D. L. Munby	Oxford
M. Scott	Oxford
E. L. Furness	Strathclyde
P. L. Cook	Sussex
N. J. Rau	University College London
J. H. Williamson	Warwick
A. Williams	York

Name	*Firm*
D. R. Anderson	British Leyland
A. F. Brazier	Dunlop
J. R. Castree	British Petroleum
E. B. Chalmers	E. B. Savory, Milln & Co.
G. C. C. Chivers	Metal Box Co.
J. F. Chown	J. F. Chown & Co.
G. Cleaver	Joseph Lucas (Electrical)
E. H. Cownie	Society of Motor Manufacturers and Traders
P. J. Cropper	Gilbert Eliot & Co.
M. Gibbs	Phillips & Drew

Name	Firm
C. B. Hill	British Leyland
E. Jones	Esso
D. F. Lomax	National Westminster Bank
J. G. Morrell	James Morrell & Associates
E. E. Pollock	British Transport Docks Board
M. J. Prag	Simon & Coates
R. Smail	Turner & Newall
L. S. Staniland	James Morrell & Associates
J. F. Sudworth	Imperial Chemical Industries
B. J. P. Woods	Guest Keen & Nettlefolds

5 'Fundamental Economics Concepts'*

In dealing with the numerous and varied economic problems that arise in real life, a small set of economics ideas or principles is applied repeatedly. An understanding of the concepts in this set is absolutely essential to an understanding of society's economic problems and how they might be solved. These concepts form an

* Part III of a report by K. G. Lumsden and R. E. Attiyeh for the Economics Education Project. Part I sets out the concept of a 'core' of 'a well-articulated and widely accepted body of tools and principles'. Part II deals with the methodology of economics. (Reproduced by permission of the authors.)

important part of the core material of a basic economics
course and are outlined in the following four sections.

(a)   *Scarcity and Choice*
       Economic problems arise when people (individuals
       or groups) want more than their resources can
       provide, i.e., when there is scarcity. To deal ration-
       ally with economic problems, it is necessary to dis-
       tinguish between wants and preferences, on the
       one hand, and resources and opportunities, on the
       other, and to understand how together they create
       the necessity for choice.
            Wants and preferences define the goals of econ-
       omic activity. Those commodities which provide
       positive welfare are things that people want. The
       terms on which people are willing to substitute or
       exchange commodities reflect their preferences.
            Resources, together with knowledge of produc-
       tive techniques, determine the set of possible com-
       binations of commodities that can be produced.
       The economic problem of choice involves finding
       the element in this set of opportunities which is
       best in terms of satisfying wants and accommodat-
       ing preferences.
            What value system (i.e., whose wants and pre-
       ferences) should prevail is a political and ethical
       question that lies outside the scope of economic
       analysis. Nevertheless, how this question is an-
       swered will have implications for economic organ-
       isation and resource allocation. For example, what
       economic institutions are most appropriate may
       depend on whether wants and preferences are to
       be individually or collectively determined. An

individualistic emphasis might require more decentralised decision making (perhaps with greater
reliance on competitive markets) and a collective
approach greater centralisation (perhaps with
greater emphasis on government planning). Given
a set of wants and preferences, the economist's
function is to predict, or to enable others to predict, how changes in economic conditions and
economic organisation will affect welfare.

(b) *Economic Efficiency*
How fully society's given wants and preferences
can be satisfied depends on how resources are allocated, i.e., some patterns of resource use are more
efficient than others. For a given value system,
three main considerations are relevant to how efficiently resources are used. First, output will be
higher the greater the rate of resource utilisation.
When resources are unemployed it will be possible
to increase output and economic welfare by putting those resources to use. Second, the degree of
economic efficiency will depend on the extent to
which technological considerations such as relative
factor endowments and resource indivisibilities
are taken into account. Only when there is specialisation in production that exploits comparative
advantages and the gains from division of labour,
will resources be allocated efficiently. Third,
economic efficiency requires that output can be
exchanged among individuals and groups both to
cater for differences in preferences and to adjust
imbalances arising from specialisation in production. That is, as long as there are possible gains

from an exchange of commodities, efficiency can be increased by carrying out such an exchange.

Full efficiency can be achieved only if, as long as the benefit (in terms of satisfying wants) from any particular use of a resource outweighs the benefit from the best alternative use (the opportunity cost), then that activity is undertaken. If this principle is consistently applied for all employment, production and exchange decisions it would be impossible to increase output by any reallocation.

(c)   *Income Distribution*

As was noted previously, whose value system shall determine the goals of economic activity is a political and ethical question. Likewise, how different individuals and groups ought to share in the net gains from economic activity also lies outside the professional competence of the economist. While the economist may be able to analyse the causes and effects of a given income distribution, it is not within the bounds of economics science to discuss the propriety of that distribution. For a given set of goals, in some circumstances, there may be a conflict between greater efficiency and more equitable income distribution. For example, a particular reallocation of resources might lead to a higher national output, but a less desirable distribution of income. Or, a policy that is intended to improve income distribution may lead to a lower national output. Depending on whose value system is being followed, it may, or may not, be preferable to make such changes.

Efficiency and equity considerations may be in conflict in yet another way. For efficiency purposes, it is necessary that a resource be put to a particular use only if its value marginal product in such employment covers its opportunity cost, i.e., only if the value of its contribution to national output exceeds the value of its contribution in any alternative activity (including leisure in the case of labour). If resource owners are self seeking, it may be necessary to pay them the value of their resources' productivity in its best use in order to get them to behave in the desired manner. This may result (particularly in cases where resources in fixed supply command payments of economic rent) in a pattern of income distribution that ranks low in society's system of values.

(d) *Aggregate Output and Income*
As indicated in Section Two, unless resources are fully utilised efficiency will not be achieved. While there are considerable difficulties involved in obtaining a single valued measure of total output, only when available resources are fully utilised will aggregate output be equal to its potential. Since the total output of goods and services is determined by the combined activities of all consumers and producers (including government) in the economy, full utilisation requires a good deal of co-ordination among economic units. If complete reliance is placed on decentralised decision making through markets, this co-ordination can be achieved only if prices in all markets, including the product, factor and money markets, adjust to

equate quantities supplied and demanded.

When market imperfections prevent full employment of resources, it is possible to compensate for discrepancies between quantities supplied and demanded by various types of monetary and fiscal policies which influence aggregate demand for output and for resources. For example, by buying or selling securities in financial markets the government can influence interest rates and, thereby, private expenditure for goods and services. The government can also encourage consumers and businesses to modify their expenditure by changing tax rates; and the government's own purchases can be expanded or contracted to secure full employment.

An added problem arises in a market economy when price changes are relied on to co-ordinate individual consumption and production decisions. Even if markets work perfectly, the result may involve substantial changes in the average price level which could cause undesired changes in income distribution. Additionally, an unstable price level could create uncertainty in the minds of decision makers about the value of money which in turn could reduce the effectiveness of the market mechanism in efficiently allocating resources. As well as promoting full resource utilisation, monetary and fiscal policy can be used to reduce instability in the price level and its concomitant effects.